Crystal Palace - Accident or Arson?

Robert H. Knowles

With additional material by
Melvyn Harrison, Chairman,
Crystal Palace Foundation

The Crystal Palace Foundation
Registered Charity No. 285563
ISBN 978-1-897754-29-0
Published in 2021 by
The Crystal Palace Foundation
Copyright © Estate of Robert H. Knowles
and The Crystal Palace Foundation 2021

IN GRATITUDE

The author is deeply grateful to the Crystal Palace Foundation, especially its present Chairman Mr. Alan J. Watson and Trustee Mr. Melvyn Harrison, for both their enthusiasm and for helping to bring this book to the notice of the publishers.

Robert Knowles, 1980.

CONTENTS

Acknowledgements

No book of this type can be the work of one man. Rather it must be the work, the thoughts, the recollections, and above all, the generosity of many people who, at the outset, receive a letter or a 'phone call from a person unknown to them, asking for help in establishing facts and gathering information. It has been the happy experience of this writer to have received help and encouragement in abundance from all but two of the dozens of organisations and individuals approached. A work such as this finds the author simply a recipient and sorter of information, which he transfers to paper in the form of words in the hope that those words will go, in some way at least, toward the solving of one problem or another. Without the many generous souls who provide the information upon which the work is based, the author is as helpless as a bird without wings. To mention by name every person who wrote to me or contacted me on the subject of this book would require too much space. I am, nonetheless, deeply grateful to them all.

Following is a list of a few to whom my special thanks and my gratitude are due.

Individuals: At the head of this list, I must surely place Mr. Albert Stone of Anerley, formerly of Penge Fire Brigade and now retired, to whom no request for help went unanswered over a long and often trying period of time, during which his optimism for the success of this enterprise and his encouragement never flagged; to Mr. Stone's son Albert, at present serving with the London Fire Brigade at Beckenham, my gratitude is due for his assistance with problems of hydraulics, and for endless encouragement; Mrs. Stone for having provided me with all the comforts of home; Mr. Stone's niece and nephew for their generous hospitality during the early and formative days of this project; the late Mr. Leslie Leete, former Chief Officer of the London Fire Brigade; Mr. W. Babington, at the time of writing Chief Officer of Kent County Fire Brigade and Mr. D. P. Bream, Station Officer London Fire Brigade, serving at Beckenham who, between them, were able to place me in touch with Mr. Stone and his son; Mr. Joseph Milner, until recently Chief Officer of the London Fire Brigade, for his endless patience and long suffering with my many requests and queries; Sir Frederick Delve, former Chief Officer of the London Fire Brigade who, in several letters, described for me his own experiences as a young Sub-Officer at the Crystal Palace fire; the late Mr. Frank Dann, of the London Fire Brigade, with special knowledge of the Crystal Palace fire who, unknown to the author, was desperately sick but nevertheless was ready to help in whatever way he could; Lady Buckland and her daughters Irene and Chrystal for their generous hospitality and to Lady Buckland for lending me a valuable and irreplaceable scrap book which belonged to her husband, and for answering many questions about Sir Henry and their years at the Crystal Palace; Mr. John Henderson of Sydenham, Manager of the Park and grounds from 1950 until his retirement in 1963, for lending the author a priceless collection of photographs and old prints, many of which were interior views of the Crystal Palace. He also enlightened the author as to the nature, character and personality of Sir Henry Buckland; Mr. B. Barkway-Jones, General Manager of Jones Brothers Department Store, Holloway, London, who very kindly let me have Lady Buckland's address; Mr. Geoff Gale of Hitchin, Hertfordshire, who provided the author with vital evidence, encouragement and friendship; Captain A. E. Middleton of Torquay,

Devon for providing a set of fine photographs of the Crystal Palace; Mrs. Phyllis Griggs of Royston, Hertfordshire for contacting the author about her father, the late Mr. Frank Tullett, who was inside the Crystal Palace when the fire started, and for providing photographs; Mr. B. Flowers of Clapham, London for offering vital evidence; Mrs. M. Sullivan of South Norwood for relating her experiences on the night of the fire and for providing evidence as to the time of the fire's outbreak; Mr. A. L. Bridger of Upper Norwood for being able to confirm Mrs. Sullivan's times; Mr. F. J. Knight of Beckenham, for photographs; Mr. Thomas Wernham of Brockley, London, for providing interesting newspaper cuttings; Mr. George Morris, of Kenley, Surrey, who was a member of the Crystal Palace Orchestra, for describing how he escaped from the Crystal Palace after the fire had got out of control; an expert in domestic gas supply and distribution, who was closely familiar with the gas services to the Crystal Palace, but for professional reasons desires to remain unnamed; the late Mr. Ford of Southend-on-Sea, for further confirmation of Mrs. Sullivan's times; Mr. S. Neale of West Wickham, Kent, for information to the effect that there were two separate fires in the Crystal Palace on the night of 30th November, 1936; Mr. H. M. Marsh of Orpington, Kent who was, for many years, a plumber at the Crystal Palace and was able to confirm for the author what the gas engineer had stated to be the location of the gas meter, and general layout of the gas services to the Palace; Professor George Chadwick, Landscape Architect and Chartered Town Planner, for allowing me to draw heavily from his fine book entitled *'The Works of Sir Joseph Paxton'* and from which my description of the waterworks at the Crystal Palace is largely taken; Mrs. E. Johnson of Clapham, London, for her interesting newspaper cuttings and kind hospitality; P. E. Manning for the interesting story about his father's visit to Gipsy Hill Police Station on 30th November 1936; Jim Barnard, a Bishopsgate fireman; George Palmer Chapman.

Press: Mr. Harry Klopper, the editor of Fire, the journal of the fire protection profession, for permission to quote from the January 1937 issue; The South London News Group, for publishing the author's letter asking for the assistance of people connected with the Crystal Palace, past or present; the Daily Mirror, for publishing the author's letter asking for the assistance of the general public; the following newspapers for permission to quote from issues for Tuesday 1st December 1936: *The Daily Mail, The Star* and *The News Chronicle* (all three becoming part of Associated Newspapers Ltd.); *The Daily Telegraph; The Daily Mirror; The Daily Express; The Daily Herald* (which became part of the Sun Group of Newspapers).

Organisations: The staff of the Greater London Council (GLC) Records Room, County Hall, London, (now London Metropolitan Archives) for their assistance with records and books and for allowing me to view their fine collection of photographs of the Crystal Palace taken before and after the fire, and for supplying a ground floor plan of the Crystal Palace indicating where the fire is thought to have started; Mr. H. D. Lilley of Chance Brothers Limited of Smethwick, for describing for the author the nature of 'Puttyless' glazing; Mr. P. T. M. Smart of H. M. Fire Research Station, Boreham Wood, who, on behalf of the then Director, Mr. Lawson, was able to assist the author as to the behaviour of inflammable liquids and solids; the County Librarian and staff of the Public Library, Stevenage, Hertfordshire, for all their help and kindness over a long period of time during which they were able to obtain a long list of books, and photocopies of newspapers; Sir Douglas Fox & Partners, Consulting Engineers, for a finely-detailed ground floor plan of the Crystal Palace; an unknown fireman serving with the London Fire Brigade Information and Public Relations Department, who was just a voice on the other end of a telephone, but nonetheless brimming over with enthusiasm and encouragement, at a time when it was much needed and when this book was just a thought and a ray of hope in the mind of the author; all the other staff of the London Fire Brigade's Public Relations Department who, from time to time, have answered various queries, and for whom nothing was too much trouble; Gas Board; Metropolitan Police; National Archives; London County Council Records Office (now London Metropolitan Archives); Department of Scientific and Industrial Research (The department was abolished by the Science and Technology Act 1965 which dispersed its functions over a number of government departments and other bodies); Firemen Remembered.

A special debt of gratitude is owed by the author to Mrs. Irene Barker of Newhaven, Sussex, formerly Mrs. Clark, for relating to the author her former husband's account of his discovery of the fire in the ladies' cloakroom at the Crystal Palace, and his efforts to contain that fire.

To my dear wife Nancy, who, although afflicted by chronic ill health, and often very tired has read every word of this manuscript offering advice and constructive criticism.

Introduction

To the very young, unless they be enlightened by reading or by parental memory, the Crystal Palace is a football team, a motor racing circuit, an athletics centre, or is on the destination indicator on one of London's red buses. For those of us who are not so young, to those of us in our 'forties and upwards, the Crystal Palace revives memories of brass bands, huge and grandiose fireworks displays, Handel Festivals and many other great classical occasions, exhibitions of all kinds and spectacular shows of every conceivable description, all set against the enchanting fairy-tale back-drop of Sir Joseph Paxton's vast glass palace on Sydenham Hill.

On the night of Monday 30th November 1936, Sir Joseph Paxton's masterpiece was burned to the ground by a mysterious fire, the cause of which has never been satisfactorily explained. Stop in the street any Londoner old enough to remember the great fire, and a count of at least three quarters of those questioned will tell you that the Crystal Palace was running at a financial loss and that the then General Manager, one Sir Henry Buckland, fired the building so as to collect the insurance money. Over the years, rumour, speculation and legend have multiplied and multiplied again about the Crystal Palace fire and Sir Henry Buckland's involvement with it; the general inference being that Sir Henry was a sinister, selfish opportunist who would stop at nothing to enrich himself. During the Second World War it was suggested that he was a German spy and held in prison as such, the rumour having arisen for no other reason than that he was absent from home for a lengthy period on what was perfectly legitimate business. So persistent did this story become that Sir Henry's wife, Lady Maud Buckland, found herself being snubbed in the street by people she had come to regard as close friends. In the end, she was forced to seek legal advice in order to put a stop to this particularly nasty and cruel piece of gossip.

In this book I have tried to place Sir Henry Buckland in his true perspective – that of a somewhat old-fashioned autocrat; something of a tyrant with a hard head for money, a man who would allow for no argument, and who usually got his own way. He was also a man of unbounded optimism and outstanding personal courage who gave the greater part of his working life to restoring and improving the Palace he loved, and to which he devoted all his waking hours.

That he fired the Palace in order to swindle the insurance company is nonsense and a gross libel. That he knew before the fire that the Crystal Palace would have to go is, I believe true, but it had to go for a reason far removed from the motivations of the run-of-the-mill fire-raiser.

Sir Henry Buckland himself did not strike the match which started the fire, because he could never have brought himself to destroy his life's work and his greatest love; so the job was left to another whose true identity may never be known. It may be that Sir Henry Buckland, whilst knowing of the intention to destroy the Palace that night, never came face to face with the person who lit the fire, nor had the slightest idea who, or what he was.

On that tragic night there were two fires. In order to avoid detection by the Palace fire and security staff it is probable that the arsonist gained access to the building by way of the basement area or the 'Paxton Tunnel' (a full description of these and their uses later). Once having gained access undetected, the fire-raiser made his way to a point inside the glass on the west front of the centre transept, and beneath the tinder-dry staging of the 'Great Orchestra' and organ. Here the first fire was lit, but because of the vigilance of a passer-by, who saw the fire in time for it to be extinguished quickly by one of the Palace firemen, the fire-raiser was temporarily thwarted, and had to quickly think of a more secluded spot to light his second fire. For this he chose a ladies' cloakroom which was located between the outer office section and the Egyptian Court, well hidden from outside but still in close proximity to the staging and organ, which provided a ready-made bonfire of enormous size. Having lit the second fire and made sure it was burning well, the fire-raiser made his escape, again, probably by the basement or the 'Paxton Tunnel', coming out either on to the High Level Railway Station, or at the entrance to the tunnel behind the old railway building in Wells Park Road, Sydenham. This building is now used as residential flats, and the entrance can still be seen at the bottom of the garden of these flats.

Chapter One

The Sydenham Crystal Palace

Before we can proceed to examine intelligently the last tragic hours in the life of the Crystal Palace, it is important that we learn something of the building itself, its origins, its structure, the general layout of its surroundings, the contents of its vast interior and their location, and the many and varied uses to which the building was put.

The Crystal Palace first saw the light of day in London's Hyde Park, where it was erected to house The Great Exhibition of the Works of Industry of All Nations in 1851. This long-winded description was to become abbreviated in time, until it became known as The Great Exhibition of 1851. The building was the brainchild of one Joseph Paxton, later to become Sir Joseph Paxton, gardener extraordinary, turned engineer and architect. Paxton designed and supervised the construction of the Hyde Park building, leaning heavily on his lengthy experience of greenhouses and forcing houses as a pattern and guide for his new structure which, when it was completed, turned out to be the biggest greenhouse the world had seen and, in all probability, would ever see. This is a pity, because it was indeed a thing of grace and much beauty. It was also the first practical demonstration of prefabricated construction as we know it today; that is, a system whereby the component parts are manufactured by various industries elsewhere and delivered in finished form to the site, there to be assembled with comparative ease. Each part may be fashioned so as to be interchangeable, not unlike a giant Meccano set. Paxton's building was constructed of iron and timber to form a huge framework which was, except for the ground floor, covered entirely with glass – as is the case with a greenhouse or conservatory. Because of the preponderance of glass, it became known as the Crystal Palace. It consisted of a flat, rectangular nave 1,848ft long, by 408ft wide, with a height of 63ft. Its central feature was an arched transept raised above the nave to a height of 108ft, with a span of 72ft. The total floor area including galleries was over 989,000sq ft, and the area of glass surfaces approximately 900,000sq ft.

The Great Exhibition was doubtless a success. If this was so with the Exhibition, it was equally so with the building in which it was which housed. From all parts of the world, people came in their thousands to cast their gaze upon the marvel in glass and iron now gracing Hyde Park. In recognition of his work on the building, Paxton was knighted by Queen Victoria in the August of 1851.

Long before the Exhibition had run its successful course, the future of Paxton's building was being widely discussed. It was never intended to be other than a temporary structure, to be dismantled at the closing of the Exhibition. However, due to its undeniable merit and world-wide acclaim, a great public clamour (much- echoed in Parliament) arose, demanding retention of the building on a permanent basis. To this clamour Paxton, naturally concerned for his brain-child, added his full weight and his formidable influence. For some time, the debate raged backwards and forwards between those for retention and those against. To retain such a huge structure in Hyde Park was impracticable; moreover, the Royal Commission responsible for having organised the Exhibition was also responsible under charter for the removal of the building and the restoration of the ground to parkland once the exhibition was closed. There was little or nothing which either Parliament or public could accomplish in the long run, except to abide by what was already obvious to the Royal Commission – that they were obliged by Royal Charter to remove the building.

The retentionists had lost completely, or so it seemed, but they had reckoned without Paxton who had, in the meantime, prepared for the inevitable. On the 13th May 1852, the formation of a new company was announced. To be called The Crystal Palace Company, it published a prospectus providing for capital of £500,000, naming Samuel Laing of the Brighton and South Coast Railway as Chairman, and Sir Joseph Paxton as a director. The new company lost no time setting about the task of purchasing the Hyde Park building from Messrs. Fox & Henderson the original contractors who, in fact, only rented the building to the Royal Commissioners. Fox & Henderson received £70,000 from the Crystal Palace Company for the building and undertook to dismantle it and re-erect it on a new site of the company's choosing. This turned out to be the grounds of Penge Place, and some adjoining land which included the summit of Sydenham Hill, its slopes already well timbered and unrestricted by any other construction. The choice of site was excellent, overlooking southeast London and having good rail access from central London, being close to the Brighton line.

Now, besides being a director of the new company Paxton was appointed its architect and engineer-in-chief, an added role and, in view of his undoubted experience, an expected responsibility, which he was quick to exploit. It was not in the nature of the man to go to so much trouble just to stage at Sydenham a mere repetition of Hyde Park; so commenced a fantastic circus whose extravagance knew no bounds, and would continue unabated for close on eighty-five years. No sooner had the columns and girders begun to arrive from Hyde Park, than Paxton began moulding them into something which was to far surpass in magnificence and splendour any previous conception.

The first column was raised to its new foundation on 5th August 1852 and construction proceeded without let-up except for occasional severe weather, and one serious accident after some scaffolding collapsed on 15th August 1853, which cost twelve lives and upset the timetable somewhat. The new building retained little of the Hyde Park design and what it did retain was generally lost because of the complexity and elaboration of the additional structure. This incorporated an arched vault running the entire 1,608ft length on an axis slightly to the east of north-south. The overall width was 312ft, the height to the springing of the vault 68ft, and to the crown 104ft. At the north and south ends of the main building were transepts each 336ft long, the width and height being the same as the main building. Wings, each 574ft long extended towards the gardens; the south wing was later connected by a glass colonnade 720ft long, 17ft wide, and 18ft high, to the low level railway station.

The commanding feature of the new building was, as at Hyde Park, the centre or main transept with its arched roof. Like everything at Sydenham, this centre transept dwarfed its predecessor at Hyde Park. Crossing the new building at right-angles on the centre-line, it was 384ft long, 120ft wide, 108ft to the springing, and 168ft to the crown of the arched vault. From the garden front the total height was, in fact, 208ft. This was because the ground fell away considerably from the west front overlooking Crystal Palace Parade (all vertical dimensions were calculated from the Parade). The garden fronts of each of the three transepts were set back inside the outer framework, hiding them in shade. This innovation was for the benefit of the foliage inside, but gave added interest and undoubted character to what otherwise would have been an immense slab wall of glass, as indeed was the case on the west front. The flooring was the same as at Hyde Park, 1½-inch-thick boards on 7-inch-thick by 2½-inch joists, on sleepers 13 inches by 3¼-inch arranged 8ft apart. The galleries had similar flooring except that there the joists and sleepers were of iron. The main framework, including all the arched vaults, was entirely of iron, all the wooden framing from Hyde Park having been dispensed with. The fabric was increased from 16-ounce to 21-ounce glass provided by Robert Lucas Chance, the Birmingham glass-maker. The total area of glass had increased considerably as compared with Hyde Park, and now amounted to 1,650,000sq.ft., this being due to the much-enlarged centre transept, the two subsidiary transepts and the arched vaulting which had become an all-embracing feature of the new building, whereas at Hyde Park it had been confined to the centre transept.

When at last the final rivets and bolts were driven home, and the ultimate pane of glass secured (there were 100,000 of them, weighing 500 tons), the result was an edifice of tremendous bulk, the unsurpassed beauty of which stemmed from an overall lightness, as though looking at a lace curtain. This effect was so pronounced as to be almost ethereal, especially when viewed in moonlight or at break of day, when droplets of dew shone like a million tiny jewels on the glass surfaces. Even the most outspoken of Paxton's critics, of whom there many, readily admitted that he had achieved a miracle in symmetry and lightness. Yet it was the effect of lightness which provoked most criticism. It was said that the structure lacked permanence and solidity. Suggestions for overcoming this came forward in profusion, the most practical being that the angles of the transepts and the nave should have been carried out in brick, terracotta, or concrete, and that the basement front overlooking the gardens should have been similarly treated up to the level of the main floor. To have so treated the angles of nave and transepts would have been to destroy Paxton's whole conception which was that of the fairy palace, a concept which he converted into fact with ability and admirable skill. One has only to look at the monstrosities in glass and concrete disfiguring London today to see where Paxton's use of glass was correct, and the critics of his work in error. It is the author's opinion however, that there is something to be said for concrete being used for the basement front up to ground floor level. This would have had the advantage of placing the building on a solid plinth without detracting from the fairy-like lace curtain effect of the whole, although Paxton's terraces did, to some extent, produce the same result.

Before proceeding with an examination of the interior of the Crystal Palace, we must digress for a while to look at the terrace gardens and waterworks. The interior arrangements at the Palace have so important a bearing on the events of 30th November 1936 that they must be constantly borne in mind when considering the final tragedy. For this reason, we must leave the interior of the building until later.

Sir Joseph Paxton's most formidable critics have accused him of gross, even reckless extravagance, when talking or writing about his work at Sydenham. When considering this accusation, one must remember that the Crystal Palace was created for the enjoyment of the masses, including the working class. Had the Palace been created to satisfy the whim of some wealthy potentate, the charge of extravagance might never have been made at all, and most certainly would never have been repeated so often. Only when something is done for the working class does one hear the cry of extravagance amplified to any degree. It is not the purpose of this book to preach class warfare; nevertheless, it is necessary, in order to view Paxton's masterpiece in proportion to its critics, to make the above observation.

It is difficult to see where the building itself was extravagant. It was a truthful building consisting only of the essentials to its existence; the foundation, supporting structure, and glass fabric. Nothing was added or superimposed to enhance the building by way of decorative gimmickry. So clever was Paxton's use of glass and iron, so very good his sense of proportion, that further embellishment would have marred rather than enhanced it.

If the charge of extravagance is valid in any respect, it could have been so only in Paxton's treatment of the grounds, and even here it is doubtful if extravagance is the correct criticism. 'Sheer impracticability' might be a much more accurate description; yet something difficult to understand and to reconcile in a man of such proven calibre.

The total area of ground used was 200 acres, purchased at cost of £67,661. It was, except for the area covered by the Palace, laid out in terracing, ornamental gardens, and parkland. The use of terracing was to a large extent dictated by the very steep slope of the ground. The upper terrace, running along the entire front of the building was 1,576ft long by 48ft wide and was reached by an imposing flight of steps in front of the centre transept; the steps were 120ft wide. Fifteen feet below the upper terrace was the garden terrace, reached by six flights of steps negotiating a steep embankment, upon which bastions were built to serve as viewing points. The garden terrace was 1,656ft long by 512ft wide, a huge area by any standards, containing formal garden features in the Italian style with flower beds, urns, statues and fountains. The whole was encompassed by an elaborate wall in which arched alcoves or niches were constructed. On top of the wall was a finely executed balustrade, tazzas and statuary. Sufficient remains of this wall, terracing and the central steps to make it well worthwhile for any serious student of Paxton's works to pay a visit to Sydenham.

The central feature of the garden terrace was a bandstand on the axis of the centre transept. From this a further flight of steps descended to a walk between trees interspersed by pools, fountains and statuary, to the Penge entrance at the eastern boundary of the park. This walk is still to be enjoyed today, although it is somewhat spoiled by a motor racing circuit which cuts across it just below the garden terrace; even so it remains, in spite of this modern desecration, a beautiful and enchanting place in which to stroll on a summer's day.

It was Paxton's intention that his system of waterworks should be the crowning glory of the Crystal Palace Park, and it was in the execution of his intent that he carried out his exercise in 'sheer impracticability'. Within the British Isles there are several places where a cliff face could be constructed, or an existing one reinforced with concrete, so as to present an unbroken perpendicular, 165ft high by three quarters of a mile long. It would then only require a veritable army of pumps to handle the water, and one would have a creditable reproduction of Niagara Falls. The cost of such a project would be enormous and the exercise pointless, because for anyone living in the British Isles wishing to see Niagara Falls there are cheap and frequent package tours to all of the world's spectacular beauty spots. This was not so in Paxton's day. There were no package tours, no cut-price jet flights, and world travel was the preserve of the wealthy and the privileged; the working masses were fortunate if they could afford a trip to Brighton on the odd summer's day. Paxton was aware of this deficiency in the Victorian social structure and his Crystal Palace was, as we shall see in due course, his way of remedying, at least in part, this deficiency. 'It is my avowed intention to bring the glories of Versailles to Sydenham so that all of London may view them.' Thus wrote Sir Joseph Paxton in a letter to a friend describing his plans for the Sydenham water displays.

Paxton's experience with the construction of waterworks was considerable. He had for many years been Head Gardener to the Sixth Duke of Devonshire and had carried out extensive waterworks at Chatsworth, the Duke's private estate in Derbyshire. These waterworks included lakes, an aqueduct and cascade, and the Emperor Fountain, so called because the Emperor of Russia was invited to watch its initial display on his visit Chatsworth in June 1844. In the event the Emperor never came, but the Great Fountain with its 270ft-high jet was still christened the Emperor, and today can be seen throwing its waters high above Chatsworth, long after the great fountains of Sydenham have vanished. The explanation is simple: – Chatsworth is blessed with a natural and copious supply of water; Sydenham on the other hand, enjoys no such advantage. There is behind the estate at Chatsworth a high escarpment of approximately 350ft. Beyond this, and elevated high above are the moors of Derbyshire, a natural collecting place for heavy rainfall, some of which finds its way in the form of streams on to the escarpment. Paxton simply dammed up one of the streams, forming a small reservoir of eight acres with an average depth of seven feet. From this, a pipe with a 15-inch bore led the water to the Emperor's nozzle 350ft below, with the overflow from the basin passing down to the river Derwent which fronts the estate.

Return pumping was not required in the driest of summers, the moorland streams and the reservoir being abundantly sufficient for Chatsworth's Emperor.

At Sydenham, there was no high escarpment and no moorland streams, the only water in the vicinity at that that time being provided by an artesian well located at the lowest point in the park. This well was a brick shaft 8ft.6 inches diameter, and 247ft in depth; Paxton added a further 328ft giving a total depth of 575ft, an entry into the chalk sub-strata considerably increasing the yield of the well. An engine raised water from this well into a reservoir which took the form of an ornamental lake extensive enough for boating. On the islands are full scale models of prehistoric monsters, still in an excellent state of preservation and, as with the terracing, well worth seeing. This lake formed the lowest level of the system and, being the water source, had the grave disadvantage of requiring expensive pumping equipment to lift water to the upper levels. Water was lifted from here to an intermediate reservoir by two 40hp engines, this being the smallest lake in the system. From here, four 40hp engines pumped water to an upper system which consisted of two high water towers, two elevated tanks and a large reservoir in the shape of a further ornamental lake at the northern end the Palace with a capacity of 6½ million gallons. To lift water from this lake to the elevated tanks and water towers, two more 30hp engines were required.

There were many fountains, pools and varied water effects within the Crystal Palace complex, but only four of these required such a huge and complicated arrangement of reservoirs, tanks and pumps for their operation. These were the temple cascades and high fountains, numbering two of each and all located in the lower part of the park. The temples, made of glass and cast iron, were no less than 70ft high, slightly higher in fact than the springing of the vault of the main building at 68ft. Each temple covered a group of statuary around which were creeping plants. Water issued from a ring around a ball, supporting a bronze figure of Mercury surmounting the dome of each temple. The water flowed over the domes, collecting inside a hollowed-out cornice, which was perforated so that a curtain of water fell over each opening, thereby covering the statuary and creeping plants with a transparent veil. The cascades ran from the foot of the temples, and consisted of broad shallow steps of sandstone. These were bordered by a range of tazzas borne by figures of children. Each culminated in a fall over an arcade into the Formal Grand Basins below, their central jets throwing water to a height of 250ft. When the full system was operating 11,788 jets used water at the enormous rate of 120,000 gallons per minute; it was first displayed in the presence of Queen Victoria on 18th June 1856.

Theoretically, in order to push water to a given height, a head supply of equal height is required. In practice however, a head supply of a somewhat greater height must be provided in order to overcome frictional losses in piping and, where exposed jets are involved, air pressure as well. To provide sufficient head supply for operating the two high fountains, Paxton had to make recourse to high water towers.

Having no personal experience of such lofty structures and the problems of wind resistance and stability associated with them, Paxton wisely obtained the services of a professional engineer of foremost repute – none other than Isambard Kingdom Brunel.

Brunel was the type of person who is with us no longer; he was an engineer in the full and complete definition of the term. During his exceedingly active life, he constructed bridges, tunnels, ships, aqueducts, steam engines and pumps, and a host of lesser works. Several of his greatest achievements remain with us, giving robust and unfailing service. The famous railway bridge crossing the river Tamar, linking Devon with Cornwall, is but one of many enduring monuments to Brunel's genius.

Brunel's design for the high, water towers at Crystal Palace was exceedingly practical, leaving nothing to beauty or to the enhancement of Paxton's creation. In time, however, they became accepted, blending in as an essential and integral part of the Palace. Dominating Sydenham Hill like a pair of giant sentinels, they served their purpose throughout the life of the Palace and, surviving the great fire outlived the Palace until, during the Second World War, some panicky bureaucrat ordered their demolition – probably because he could not sleep at night plagued by visions of German bombers using the towers as landmarks and bearing-points for their fury. On such reckoning, St. Paul's and Big Ben may have been lost forever.

The north tower was 284ft high, the south tower a fraction higher at 293ft. 8in. Both were cylindrical in shape, and rested upon foundations of concrete and brick into which were set twenty-four cast-iron columns arranged in pairs. The space between each pair of columns was covered with glass set into ten frames, which formed windows on the full circumference, and on each of the ten floors. The floors themselves were of timber, resting on wrought-iron brackets. At the top of each tower was to be found the reason for their existence – huge tanks containing 240,000 gallons of water, weighing 1,400 tons and giving a pressure at ground level of 100lbs per square inch. The tanks were dome-shaped and thirty-eight feet deep.

Besides supplying the high fountains and water temples, the tanks provided water by way of eight-inch mains to operate hydraulic blowers for two concert organs, two lifts, and six sets of hydraulic air compressors supplying forty-nine fire hydrants and sprinklers. The north tower had a public observation gallery built outside the water tank and reached by stairs or a lift; it was also sited some distance from the Palace but close to the high-level reservoir. The south tower was sited very close to the Palace, but separated from it by a collection of small wooden outbuildings. Shortly we shall learn how Paxton made use of Brunel's towers, adapting them in a most unusual and brilliant way.

The interior of the Crystal Palace was vast and complex. As with the exterior, Paxton remained true to his principle of avoiding any unnecessary ornamentation and superfluous addition which was not a structural requirement to the building's ability to remain standing and weatherproof.

If we look at a plan of the ground floor starting left to right, i.e. south to north, we are struck by a hotchpotch of seemingly uncoordinated outbuildings. These, as indicated above, were small and of wooden construction, consisting mainly of kitchens, stores and yards, and our interest in them is confined to the threat they posed to the south tower during the great fire; so we will forget them for the moment and commence our tour by entering the building proper by way of the south transept. One's first impression was of limitless space and lightness. The rows of slender vertical columns, finished in black with rich gold cornices, soared upwards for 68ft from where the great arched ribs of the vault took flight in a perfect semi-circle, to bridge the whole with a roof which had the exquisite beauty of intricate lace.

Natural light is the most efficient and the most beautiful source of illumination; the interior of the Crystal Palace gave it full play. Because of its transparency the changing weather created a multitude of colour effects, which were projected and reflected through thousands of glass panes. The sun's rays on a bright day and the moonlight on a clear night added their own tracery to Paxton's wizardry. The haunting beauty of the south transept in dark shadow with the moonlight reflected in the spray from the Crystal Fountain was a vision of what the poets might imagine to be heaven. The sound of water falling softly into the fountain pool was as the music of invisible angels, at times appearing in solid form as the moon in its eternal traversing across the void would shed its ethereal light on to one after another of the marble statues, touching them as if by the magic of some fairy wand, and bringing them to life.

The Crystal Fountain was designed and built by Follett Abraham Osler using pure ground and polished glass. It stood 27ft high and weighed four tons, its basin being of polished marble adorned with delicate statuary. Added interest was provided by the inclusion in the pool of rare tropical plants and fish, demanding careful temperature control. It is now generally accepted that Osler's Crystal Fountain was one of the world's finest examples of the glassmaker's art equalled only by Max Ingrand's fountains in the Rond-Point des Champs Elysées in Paris.

As a backdrop to the Crystal Fountain, and surrounding it on three sides, was a magnificent screen executed in wood and bronze, in which was carved all the Kings and Queens of England in life-size form. Above this, and almost filling the arched vault, was the Great Clock suspended from the roof. This massive timepiece had a face 40ft in diameter and a minute hand 19ft long. The screen and clock together were the most southerly internal appointments of the south transept, forming and covering the end wall inside the glass cladding.

The entrance to the main building or nave commenced immediately to the north of the Crystal Fountain, and was about 440ft long up to its intersection with the centre transept on the south side. It continued on the north side for a similar distance up to its intersection with the north transept. The nave itself was a through walk, interspersed with pools, statuary and plants of the exotic tropical variety, forming a vast winter garden.

On each side of the nave were wide receding tiers, and inside these tiers or side aisles were to be found the series of eastern and period courts for which the Palace was famous, and by which Paxton endeavoured to bring to the ordinary person a glimpse of the world which lay beyond the narrow confines of a dingy, back-to-back terraced Victorian slum in London's East End.

The courts were in part original, brought at great expense from abroad, in part beautifully executed reproductions, and all constructed and laid out to full scale. They were nine in number, and described thus: the Chinese Court, the Egyptian Court, the Greek Court, the Roman Court, the Alhambra Court, the Byzantine Court, the Renaissance Court, the Japanese Garden Court, and Pugin's English Mediaeval Court. There was also a magnificent reproduction of the Bay of Naples, viewed from the terrace of a full-scale replica Pompeian house. The side aisles contained types of entertainment including an electric theatre, which was the fore-runner of the cinema, amusement arcades, and the Crystal Palace Club. All these various attractions were well served with refreshment rooms and bars.

For the most part, the series of historical and period courts were grouped in the side aisles of the northern half of the nave; the original nine courts were extended in time to include an Assyrian Court and an Italian Court. To the Egyptian Court there was added a faithful copy of the Tomb of Beni Hassan; likewise, to the Alhambra Court there was added a Court of Lions. The workmanship was exquisite throughout the entire collection, and the authenticity gave the visitor a true impression of the architecture, culture and history of all these ancient civilisations, bringing to the ordinary people some knowledge of a world which, at that time, only the wealthy and privileged could afford to see at first hand.

The centrepiece of the north nave was a series of bronze fountains, so described because the fountainheads and the nymphs which surrounded them were wrought of solid bronze. The fountain basins were of marble and contained plants providing shade for a variety of freshwater fish. The dominant feature of the whole northern section was the north transept with its reproduction of the Colossi of Abu Simbel made of concrete and plaster cast, and standing on an enormous and intricately-carved and decorated plinth. The twin figures of the Colossi were 65ft high, representing perfectly the originals which are to be seen in the Temples of Rameses in Egypt – the subject of much publicity when they were successfully rescued from the rising waters of the Aswan High Dam and resited on higher ground.

Surrounding the Colossi was the tropical section containing some of the world's rarest plant species, an aviary of exotic tropical birds, and the bark of a Wellingtonia gigantea transported from Sierra Nevada; this tree grows to a height of 300ft. The side aisles accommodated an extensive library of rare books and many original manuscripts, a gallery of naval architecture, a reading room and the Queen's Apartments.

We must now retrace our steps down the north nave to the very centre of the complex. It was here that the centre transept cut at right angles across the main building, dominating it and providing the main focal point. The western end of this transept overlooked Crystal Palace Parade, and was entirely taken up by the Grand Orchestra, seating 4,000 persons on a vast semi-circle. This was built up in tiers to form a terrace and stage at the summit of which, and making the centre-piece of the whole, was the Great Organ. Built by Gray & Davison it was one of the finest concert instruments to be found anywhere in the world. It had 4,568 speaking pipes, and was originally blown by water, although it was eventually converted to electric blowing. An idea of the size of this huge stage and auditorium can be gauged from the fact that it occupied the full 120ft width. Over it all was a richly painted and gilded false ceiling made of timber, and suspended from the vault springing 108ft above floor level. Concealed within the vault were the various mechanical contrivances associated with the handling of scenery and lighting fixtures. Beneath the tiered stage were dressing rooms and storage space. Flanking it on each side were corridors leading to the crush hall and main entrance.

The point to be borne in mind is that the entire structure of the Grand Orchestra, from floor to ceiling, and from wall to wall and contained within the iron and glass fabric of the Palace itself, was one huge pile of timber, much of it light and flimsy e.g. the organ and false ceiling. So far as the events of 30th November 1936 are concerned, here was a ready-made bonfire of alarming proportions; nor was this all. On the southeast side of the transept there was a concert hall able to seat 2,000 people, and on the northeast side an opera theatre with close on 4,000 seats and containing a second organ, this one built by Walker. Both of these subsidiary halls were, for the most part, of timber construction and would create more fuel in the event of a fire in the centre transept. All of the accumulation of dry and flimsy timber added up to an appalling situation wherein it was possible, if all three halls were in use simultaneously, for upwards of 10,000 people to be encircled in a gigantic fire trap; a situation which would not be permitted today, and would not have been permitted in 1936 had the Crystal Palace stood within the area administered by the then London County Council. As it was, the Palace stood just outside the London County border and was in fact in Kent, a circumstance which was to be the recipe for disaster.

On the eastern or garden front of the centre transept, and running its full width of 120ft, there was a glazed corridor known as the Garden Lobby. Part of this was used as a restaurant, to become celebrated as the place where the royal families of many lands, as well as our own, were to partake of refreshment whilst gracing the Palace with their presence. The auspicious Garden Lobby was reached by a wide, white marble staircase descending from the main floor level of the transept. Behind the staircase and in the front of the basement were the kitchens and stores which served the restaurant. Before looking at the basement, and in order to complete our tour of the Palace proper, mention must be made of the two galleries running around the interior of the nave and transept. The upper gallery was at a level with the springing of the arched vault; it had a width of 8ft., and access was by spiral stair from the lower gallery, but it was little used by the public, its primary function being a working platform for the general maintenance of the higher parts of the building; trap doors in the sides gave access to the roof. The lower gallery was 24ft wide and was connected to the ground floor by wide straight flights of wooden stairs. Mention has already been made of the fact that the garden fronts of all three transepts were set back inside the outer framework forming recesses which, among other things, allowed the lower gallery to traverse outside the transepts, thus forming an observation platform sheltered by the overhanging roofs.

We have already seen that the ground falls away in a steep slope from Crystal Palace Parade towards the lower park. Crystal Palace Parade is the summit of what is loosely termed Sydenham Hill, although the actual hill of that name flanks the Parade at its northern end, with Anerley Hill at its southern extremity. For those who would split hairs, the Crystal Palace stood between the two hills on a ridge linking Anerley with Sydenham. Paxton desired his Palace to have its main or ground floor on a level with the ridge or summit, so that the entire building stood above the highest point of land dominating and overlooking all other features. Because of the steep fall away from the ridge, a basement was unavoidable if monstrous expense were to be avoided. As we shall see later, it required a Second World War to provide enough rubble to fill in and level up Paxton's basement.

Undoubtedly, the most interesting feature of the basement was the Paxton Tunnel and its offshoots. This tunnel ran the length of the Palace; it was a brick shaft 24ft wide, and its purpose was twofold. It enclosed the central heating system for the whole complex, and an access railway for heavy exhibition material, stage props, scenery and the like. The central heating system was made up of twenty-two boilers arranged in pairs at equal spacing along the basement, each boiler holding 11,000 gallons of water. Four, 9-inch diameter pipes linked the boilers – two flow and two return; the length of one flow and return was 1¾ miles. The total length of heating pipes of all kinds added up to close on fifty miles. Five extra boilers were added later, these being needed to maintain constant temperatures for the tropical plants and the fish in some of the fountain basins.

Waste products, fumes, hot gases and soot from the furnaces of twenty-seven boilers take a lot of disposal, and the easiest and obvious method would be to run flues straight up from the boilers to chimneys on the roof. On a building like the Crystal Palace a row of smoking chimneys would turn a fairy glass palace in to an ugly factory or like structure; this was unthinkable. To avoid this, Paxton gave full range to his brilliant ingenuity; he connected up his twenty-seven boilers to two horizontal flues, one running north, one running south along the basement and into the base works of the two water towers. From this point the flues became vertical, running straight up through the centre of the towers and their water tanks. The only visible clue to the flue outlets was a slight flat-topped protuberance on the domed roof of the towers.

The basement also contained extensive storage facilities including a good wine cellar as well as staff mess rooms, the Terrace Café, the entrance hall from the gardens with its wide marble stairway and wrought-iron banister ascending to the first floor. Also to be found in the basement were the essential services vital to all large buildings – paint shop, joiners' shop, engineers' shop, the electricity substation and, of primary importance (since in the end it became for most the scape-goat) the gas distribution system, a detailed description of which will follow in due course. On the west front of the Palace, alongside the Parade, stood several small structures of timber and galvanised sheeting used as offices and small workshops by the maintenance personnel. Included in these outbuildings was a gas compressor house, which we will examine along with the gas distribution system. There was also a fire station which, for a time, housed a Merryweather Shand Mason steam fire engine manned by the Palace firemen.

Crystal Palace Parade is, of course, still with us today; it is a fine stretch of straight and (even by today's standards) very wide roadway, lined on both sides with trees. In Paxton's day it surely must have been something of a wonder in road engineering and, like the Palace gardens, shows clearly how Paxton became influenced by Paris and Versailles although, on the Parade, the presence of London's familiar red buses destroys the illusion. In Victorian times the whole district was essentially open country. Because of the presence of the Palace and its ever-increasing popularity a gradual building up began, the district becoming a fashionable place in which to take up residence in the many fine houses which were built. Alas, today, with the disappearance of the Palace the fine houses have in many instances become dilapidated and converted into flats and tenements, rendering them just one more instance of London's ever-increasing urban sprawl.

Chapter two

The years between: a brief resumé

There were two distinct periods in the life of the Crystal Palace. They were the years from its completion in the summer of 1854 until the bankruptcy of the Crystal Palace Company in the spring of 1911 and the years following, when the Palace was governed by a Trusteeship which was formed to preserve the Palace for the nation. Our purpose is with the second period, that of the Trusteeship; however, a short resumé of the first period has its place if only to preserve continuity.

The commencement of summer 1854 saw the completion of Paxton's work, and the fulfillment of his dream. His conception in crystal glass was a reality standing atop Sydenham Hill, where on a clear day it was visible from all over London, shining like some exquisite jewel. On the 10th June 1854, the Crystal Palace was officially declared open to the public by Queen Victoria, accompanied by her husband the Prince Consort and their children and in the presence of the King of Portugal and his brother the Duke of Oporto. Included in this glittering assembly were the Duchess of Kent and Princess Mary of Cambridge, and the Lord Mayors of London, Dublin, and York. On declaring the Palace open Queen Victoria said: 'It is my earnest wish and hope that the bright anticipations which have been formed as to the future destiny of the Crystal Palace may, under the blessing of Divine Providence, be completely realised, and that this wonderful structure and the treasures of art and knowledge which it contains, may long continue to elevate and interest as well as to delight and amuse the minds of all classes of people.'

Sir Joseph Paxton had taken up residence in an English mansion-type house called 'Rockhills', which was situated to the north of the Palace. From here he watched over and supervised his masterpiece, leaving it only when called to attend to other enterprises – of which he had several. Doubtless his Crystal Palace was his greatest love. There is no doubt also that his devotion to it, and the constant worry which its financial decline caused him, sapped his health to such an extent that at dawn, on the 8th June 1865 he died, slipping quietly away without pain and within sight of his beloved creation, which was visible from his bedroom window.

Paxton's body was removed from 'Rockhills' to Chatsworth and thence to Edensor Churchyard, where he was laid to rest in a grave close to that of his lifelong and dearest friend the Sixth Duke of Devonshire, whom he had first met as a humble gardener.

'Rockhills' is now gone; only its foundations remain, covered in weeds. Its last occupant was the last General Manager of the Crystal Palace, one Sir Henry Buckland, of whom we shall learn more later.

As an attraction the Crystal Palace was a success. By 1911 and the bankruptcy, 82,000,000 people had paid for entrance, but financially it was unsound from the beginning. The Company was founded with a capital of £500,000, yet the final expenditure was £1,300,000 accounted for thus; the building £235,240, the water towers and heating equipment £123,532, the hydraulic works £80,085, the park and related outside works, more than the building at £340,231. The remainder was spent on internal decoration and exhibits. In itself the over- expenditure was not serious and not unusual because, as is often case with very large and prominent ventures, the original capital issue was heavily over-subscribed. For the eventual fiscal crash three factors were responsible; they were the high cost of maintaining the building and grounds, the lavishness of the spectacles which were staged, and the Sabbatarians who were successful in keeping the Palace closed on Sundays, the one day when the working classes were free to visit it. In those times one worked six days a week, twelve or fourteen hours a day and spent Sunday in church redeeming one's sins which, if committed at all must have been something of an achievement considering the short time available after such long hours of work.

So far as the lavishness of the spectacles is concerned, a detailed description is outside the scope of this book and, for those interested, I would refer them to the fine publication entitled 'The Crystal Palace' by Patrick Beaver. It is sufficient for our purpose to know that as the years passed the events staged grew in their extravagance but, although drawing huge crowds, the revenue obtained failed to justify the enormous outlay required.

The high cost of maintaining the whole massive complex was first highlighted by the shutting off of the garden water displays, except on special occasions. The steam pumps for lifting water to the high reservoir, tanks and water towers proved unreliable and in continual need of attention. Eventually, temple cascades and the two high fountains had to be abandoned, thus proving the impracticability of Paxton's concept with water at Sydenham. To be fair to Paxton however, stress must be laid on the fact that many of the smaller fountains – those on the terracing and inside the Palace – were in almost constant use and operating perfectly until the end in 1936. It was soon to become evident that the building itself, if it was to remain standing, would require continuous and costly attention. The English climate played havoc with the acres of glass, which cracked and broke particularly on the roofs. The iron framework rusted, demanding endless chipping and repainting. The glazing and ironwork between them had to be preserved by a permanently employed army of glaziers and painters. The wage bill for this work, an almost intolerable burden in itself, damaged the Company's resources and drove Paxton close to distraction. But worse was to come.

On the 30th December 1866, fire broke out in the north transept. Being a Sunday, the building was closed and deserted save for one solitary watchman, (on weekdays three watchmen were on duty day and night). The fire started in a paint store and spread rapidly. The lone watchman must have also acted rapidly, and with commendable presence of mind in calling the fire brigade promptly, because the major part of the building was saved. Even so, the damage was serious and, in some respects, disastrous.

The entire north transept along with its contents was destroyed, and the north nave with its Period Courts badly damaged by heat and smoke. The fire was stopped short of the great centre transept. All that remained of the north transept were the huge twin figures of the Colossi of Abu Simbel standing gaunt and scarred, rearing their battered heads 65ft high out of the pathetic debris of twisted iron and molten glass. Completely destroyed were the Alhambra, Byzantine and Romanesque Courts, the Queens Apartments, the library with its rare and irreplaceable collection of books and original manuscripts, the gallery of naval architecture, the aviary with all its birds, and all the plants in the tropical section. The total damage was estimated at £150,000. The cause of the fire was never ascertained; there was no reason to suspect arson, therefore it can only be assumed to have been accidental. It may have been caused by the spontaneous combustion of rags soaked in linseed oil or thinners, this being a frequent cause of fire in paint shops if the house-keeping is not all that it should be; a hazard that the public unfortunately knows too little about. We must, at this point, draw comparison between the fires of 1866 and 1936. The first incident involved a highly inflammable paint store producing a very serious and fierce fire at the outset, with only one man on security watch. Fire brigades in 1866 had, at best, horse-drawn steam pumps, yet the major part of the Palace was saved. The final incident of several affecting the main building, the fire of 1936, commenced in a staff lavatory. Fire brigades in 1936 had advanced both in equipment and in technique, to a degree out of all recognition to what existed in 1866, yet the whole Palace was destroyed. No reflection of an uncomplimentary kind is intended here on the actions of the fire brigades concerned with the 1936 fire; their conduct was, in all respects, in keeping with the highest traditions of what in this country has always been a very fine service, within the limitations of the technical and scientific knowledge available at any given time. The blame for the 1936 disaster lay elsewhere, but the comparison is obvious. In 1866, a serious and fierce fire from the outset with one man on security watch; in 1936, a small, insipid fire in a staff lavatory with little in close proximity of an inflammable nature, and with three men on security watch, two of whom, along with others, are known to have seen the fire while it was still confined to the lavatory.

The north transept was beyond repair, the iron framework having collapsed completely. Although the fire had spread into the north nave and ruined much of its contents, the structure remained standing, with much of the glass gone and the rest cracked and blackened by heat and smoke. An expert survey of the north nave revealed no serious structural damage, so it was cleaned and re-glazed. The fire brought forth a tremendous wave of public sympathy and cash poured in to pay for restoration. It required close on two years to restore the north nave and its contents to their original glory. The north transept itself was never rebuilt because of money difficulties and so, as can be clearly seen from photographs, the Palace appeared to be cut off short and left unfinished at its northern end thereafter.

In due course, the Palace was reopened, and the fireworks displays, which were first put on in 1865 by Charles Thomas Brock were revived, and elaborated in size and complexity, becoming world famous. The Handel Festivals, first staged in 1859, were also revived, with a chorus and orchestra of 4,000. The problem of the building's maintenance continued as a never-ending drain on the Company's resources, the crux of the trouble being the great centre transept. Because of its height in relation to the much lower naves, it was more exposed to the weather; the huge arched roof was especially vulnerable to damage in high winds, which are well known for their ferocity by anyone who is familiar with Sydenham. A combination of these and driving rain in winter dislodged the putty which held the glass in place and which, in the heat of summer become dry and cracked. Eventually things became so bad as to render this important roof dangerously insecure; the whole thing was leaking every time it rained and glass was breaking and falling out of place making it unsafe for anyone underneath.

During the summer of 1899, the entire roof, covering 100,000sq.ft., was renewed with 'puttyless' glazing, the work being carried out by Messrs. Mellowes & Co. of Sheffield.

During the following winter, in spite of severe wind and rain, not a single pane of glass was broken or dislodged and the interior of the transept remained perfectly dry. Messrs. Mellowes & Co.'s 'puttyless' glazing was an undisputed success; it also produced a bonus which enhanced considerably the internal lightness of the structure, and the clean fine-lined appearance of the exterior.

As other attractions gained ground, in a world changing with a swiftness unknown in recorded history, so the popularity of the Crystal Palace waned and the financial account sank deeper into the red. By 1911, the situation had reached the threshold of bankruptcy. Coincidence had it that 1911 was also the year of King George V's Coronation. The Crystal Palace Company decided the time appropriate for a last gamble to save the sinking ship, and the Palace put on the greatest show of its career. This was the Festival of Empire which attempted the reconstruction of the British Empire in miniature. Three-quarter-sized replicas of all the Commonwealth Parliament buildings constructed with timber and plaster were set up in the grounds, and stocked with products representative of the appropriate countries. Further attractions included an Indian tea plantation, a South African diamond mine and a Canadian logging camp. The whole was connected up by a miniature railway with live steam locomotives. Inside the great centre transept, lavish concerts and other entertainments were staged, employing the services of many of the world's finest artistes. At the closure of the Festival hundreds of thousands of people had paid for admission, but to no avail.

In the winter of the same year the Crystal Palace Company was declared bankrupt and a High Court Order was issued for the sale by public auction of the entire property and its contents. The auction was due to take place at the Estate Rooms, 20, Hanover Square, London, W1 on 28th November 1911. The auctioneers were Messrs. Knight, Frank, & Rutley, the Palace and grounds being offered for sale as a going concern: 'a freehold estate of 200 acres, 3 roods, 22 poles', as one lot. The sale was announced by The Times on 11th September 1911. A huge number of letters and articles appeared in the press, financial donations flowed in and The Lord Mayor of London organised a conference to discuss the matter. On the 9th November 1911 The Times triumphantly announced 'THE CRYSTAL PALACE SAVED'. Lord Plymouth, Lord Lieutenant of Glamorgan and Mayor of Cardiff, a man of considerable public spirit whose motive was to save the Palace for the nation, had put a deposit down of £200,000. With that money and all the donations, the High Court allowed a contract to be drawn up between the vendors (Knight, Frank and Rutley) and Lord Plymouth in full and final settlement for the sum of £210,000.

The problem for Lord Plymouth was what to do with his acquisition. In 1913, a Lord Mayor's Fund came to his rescue; Lord Plymouth received his deposit back and the Palace became the property of the nation, to be preserved and administered by a charity and run by trustees. Within a few months the country was engulfed, with the rest of Europe, in a war which was to last for four dreadful years. Except for use as a naval depot, the Palace lay forgotten and deteriorating.

Chapter three

The Palace restored

November 1918 saw the weary and unsatisfactory conclusion of 'the war to end all wars'. With over 38,000,000 dead or maimed, the world was sick of war, and the carnage following in its wake. In all parts of the world men's minds became preoccupied with peace among nations, and statesmen, victorious and vanquished alike, wrestled with the daunting problem of how to make peace and make it lasting.

It was against this background of disillusionment, bitterness, and grievous uncertainty for the future that the Trustees of the Crystal Palace set about their mammoth task of restoration. The first essential was already accomplished; the finding of a man capable of undertaking the control and direction of what was, without exaggeration, a seemingly impossible task. The man chosen by the Trustees was well versed in achieving the seemingly impossible. In 1905, an unknown department store manager caught a train from London to Harrogate, where he presented himself to the Borough Corporation of the Yorkshire resort informing its members that, under his management, the Royal Spa establishments would, within twelve months, cease to be a burden on the rates. His name was Henry James Buckland, and the sorely-pressed Corporation took him at his word, although they were sceptical of his ability to honour it; no one had been able to do it before, and so it had come to be considered impossible. Twelve months later, Henry James Buckland had confounded the sceptics. The Royal Spa was 'off the rates' and within two years was showing a profit. The impossible had become the possible, and the one-time store manager was accepted as something of a genius.

Nine years were to pass before Henry Buckland was to return to London to inform the Trustees of the Crystal Palace that their mountain of cracked and broken glass could be completely restored and made financially sound. Like Harrogate, London was sceptical but, meanwhile, the Trustees were becoming desperate over the problem of how to breathe life back into their building. Madmen were hard to come by outside of a lunatic asylum, and if Henry Buckland was mad enough to lay his head on the chopping block, then let him, and hope that by some miracle he might keep his head and save the Crystal Palace. It was easy to understand the sceptic. The old Crystal Palace Company, launched on over-optimism, had foundered on the same ingredient and here, in 1914, with war just round the corner, was another super-optimist promising the impossible. Desperate, anxious, and in a few cases cynical, the Trustees were nevertheless, men of high principle imbued with but one desire – to carry out the saving and restoration of the Palace so that it would, in due course, become London's finest showpiece; and an object truly worthy of the nation to which it now belonged.

Henry James Buckland took over at Sydenham in 1914. Because of the outbreak of war and associated material restrictions, any major work on the building was out of the question for four years. It was offered to and accepted by the Admiralty as a training base for the Royal Naval Volunteer Reserve, Royal Naval Air Service and Royal Naval Division officers and men, to become officially known as H.M.S. Victory. 125,000 men were to receive their initial training there before the conclusion of hostilities. The Palace was given to the Admiralty rent-free, so there was virtually no income for the period of the Navy's tenure. Once vacated by them restoration began in earnest.

The entire building and its contents were, for the most part derelict. The famous historical courts presented a sorry sight, with chipped and broken plaster and peeling paint. Everywhere, broken glass rendered the structure unsafe. The grounds were a forest of weeds, the fountain basins dried up, filled with rubbish and completely unworkable. The job facing the new general manager was daunting, to say the least. Being of a practical turn of mind, he was quick to realise that the primary requirement was to start cash flowing in quickly by reopening to the public within the shortest possible time.

The south nave and transept being uncluttered except for statuary, this was obviously the easiest section for rapid repair and redecoration. Bank overdrafts totalling £60,000 were obtained and because of Henry Buckland's shrewd management and respect for the value of money they proved to be the last overdrafts asked for.

Messrs. Mellowes & Company were once more commissioned to re-roof the south nave and transept with their well-proven 'puttyless' glazing. The ironwork was cleaned of rust and repainted. The statuary was taken in hand and piece-by-piece carefully restored by experts, and certain preliminary work was carried out in the great centre transept. By 1920 it was possible to reopen to the public. The north nave with its historical courts remained for the time being closed off, out of bounds and desolate.

The show which Henry Buckland devised for the reopening demanded a degree of courage of a high order, because it constituted a very heavy gamble with public feeling and sentiment; the war had been concluded but two years, and the memory of its appalling horror, its staggering loss of life pain and suffering was still fresh in people's thoughts. Hospitals all over Europe were still overcrowded with the human wreckage of bloody conflict. The makers of armaments, the great industrialists, Krupp, Schneider-Creusot, Vickers Armstrong, Ansaldo and Skoda were no longer looked upon as the Gods of technical advancement. The name of Krupp in particular had become abhorred – to the point where the very mention of it produced an impassioned response of hatred, unsurpassed in recent history.

It was in the face of such adverse sentiment that Henry Buckland made his gamble and crammed the south nave and transept with an exhibition of war material. The exhibition included everything from rifles to 16-inch naval guns; from field pieces to tanks and aircraft, and even to model mock-ups of the most gruesome battle scenes. On the 9th June 1920, this gigantic emporium of death and destruction was declared open by King George V and Queen Mary, to become the first home of the Great Victory Exhibition, later removed to the building today known as the Imperial War Museum.

The exhibition was very popular from the moment of opening to final closure. Four years later, 5,000,000 people had paid for admission to the Crystal Palace war exhibition, and Henry Buckland's gamble had become an odds-on winner. The reasons for this idiosyncrasy in human behaviour is best left to the psychologist.

The feast of destructive power was garnished with a sweetener. Alongside the guns, tanks, bombs and shells the industrialists, with an eye to peace and plenty, and no doubt conscious of the need to restore their image as men of progress and human advancement, showed off a varied range of consumer goods, including electric washing machines and vacuum cleaners. One well-known manufacturer of armour plate had a full-page advert appearing in the commemorative booklet entitled 'From War to Peace' depicting battleships giving place to luxury liners, and tanks replaced by motor cars. Here indeed were swords turning into ploughshares.

Two incidents, both fires, were to mar the period of the exhibition. During the first year, fire destroyed the stage and ceiling of the Palace Theatre and broke through the glass roof, which was considerably damaged in the area above the Theatre. On the 23rd February 1923, a small fire damaged war exhibits in the south transept. Both outbreaks were controlled without undue difficulty by the Palace Fire Brigade, and no outside help was called for.

During the same period the great centre transept became the scene of major engineering work. Immediately upon conclusion of the war the entire structure of the Palace was rigorously inspected for defect. Except for broken glass and surface rust the only serious defect uncovered was in the east, or garden elevation of the centre transept. This consisted of the tubular cast iron columns which formed the uprights, and the arch which spanned them. The columns were formed from a number of tubes set one upon the other and bolted through at the flanges where wooden packing pieces were inserted, presumably to blank off the inside of the tubes from rain water. Because of some oversight the wooden packing pieces were not weather treated and, as a result, they had rotted, causing the tubes to settle upon each other unevenly until the whole look was a zigzag appearance; the full variation from the vertical, was 6 inches in the outward direction, and about 3½ inches inwards. To have stripped down and rebuilt the columns and arch would have required the removal of the roof, or the erection of temporary support, both involving costly expense and the risk that, once disturbed, the old columns may have disintegrated if advanced corrosion was found.

It was decided, therefore, to erect a steel latticework brace behind the original columns and arch, bolting the latter to the new steelwork so that, in effect, it was transferring its own weight and load-bearing to the new steelwork. The work was designed by Mr. Wright (who was at that time the very able resident engineer), in conjunction with Sir Douglas Fox & Partners, who acted as consulting engineers. It was commenced during the summer of 1920, and completed during the following summer. A full technical description of this important renovation accompanied by drawings can be found in 'Engineering', 20th April 1921. Before the Crystal Palace war exhibition had run its full four years, the unseen storm conditions of worsening international relations were over the horizon and shaping up into ominous clouds heavy with grim potential.

Possessed with a tremendous self-assurance and a dynamic optimism for the future, Henry Buckland bent himself more and more towards promoting the success and the well-being of what, for him, was the most important building in the entire universe. In all truth he had donned the mantle of Sir Joseph Paxton.

After the war exhibition had moved to its new home, Buckland turned the south transept into a permanent centre for exhibitions of every conceivable kind. Along with the exhibitions, he promoted annual events such as dog shows, cat shows and bird shows which were soon to become of international repute and status for animal lovers. As money came in at a steady pace and bank overdrafts were repaid, Buckland was able to turn his mind to the refurbishing of the great centre transept and the historical and period courts which occupied so much of the north nave.

The great centre transept was traditionally the home of classical entertainment; to mention the Handel festivals is to recall to mind but one of the more notable of many of the finest musical performances ever staged in Britain. The essential to most of these performances was the Great Organ. This instrument had probably been used more continuously and worked harder during its long life than any organ of similar type. It was therefore in need of major attention. After much careful thought and expert consultation, it was decided to have the organ completely rebuilt by Messrs J. W. Walker & Sons. 'Discus' fan blowers replaced the old hydraulic blowers, the pitch of the instrument was lowered, and nearly five miles of new piping was installed. The number of speaking pipes was slightly reduced, and now numbered 3,714. The cost of rebuilding was £9,000 – and worth every penny. The Crystal Palace could now boast the finest concert organ that acoustic engineering could conceive.

By the 1930s the Crystal Palace was showing its age, leaking at the joints and succumbing to rust and weather. The cracked gutters and glass panes had earlier been caulked with pitch, thus introducing another fire risk. The transept itself was reglazed, redecorated and reseated with more comfortable chairs. The catering facilities were modernised and enlarged and some attempt was made to improve the heating, but for reasons of the building's unusual construction this was not all that successful. Nevertheless, at long last this important part of the Palace was able once more to take its rightful place at the very summit of London's entertainment offering. The Handel Festivals were revived along with various other delights, and the Crystal Palace became a great classical mecca for thousands of music lovers.

It is a fact that of the many existing art forms, classical music is not lucrative in terms of monetary gain, and is likely to produce a loss. Classical music venues are dependent on a benevolent establishment whether it be national or local except that at the Crystal Palace, not one penny of Government or any other subsidy was received, leaving Henry Buckland to struggle unaided as best he could. Here indeed, was courage; and shame too. The courage of a man who could lose £3,000 on one Handel Festival and still smile and continue to put on another and yet another similar performance; the shame of an establishment which turned its back and looked the other way while a nation's architectural gem and cultural Olympus struggled to survive.

In order to continue with classical festivals, which he was determined to do, Henry Buckland used the centre transept from time to time for more popular wide appeal pursuits such as boxing and wrestling, always making sure that the contestants were of top class and sure to draw capacity crowds. Another highly successful crowd-puller was the Christmas circus for which Buckland scoured Europe, booking only the best acts of the day. With such innovations he was able to offset his Festival losses and thus continue to cater for a wide variety of tastes.

His major headache now was the north nave and its desolate historical and period courts. By great good fortune he had on his staff a tradesman painter and decorator with more than average artistic talent, one Peter Lewer. Almost single-handedly and taking many years of painstaking effort Peter Lewer, gradually, and with meticulous care, restored the courts to their original glory. To add to the attractions of the north nave, room was found for a modern cinema to replace the old electric theatre and further room was allocated to the Crystal Palace Billiard Club, giving space for forty full-size tables – surely a record under one roof.

All work on the north transept, including reglazing and renovation of the bronze fountains, was completed by spring 1935, when this part of the Palace was reopened to the public by H.R.H. The Duke of Kent. Also fully restored, and now illuminated by means of neon tubes and multi-stage flashers, was Osler's Crystal Fountain. By this time, the gardens and park had been considerably cleaned up as well. The fountains along the terraces were all working once more and the system of lakes were cleaned and fully operative. Paxton's water temple cascades and high fountains however remained abandoned as impractical of restoration.

The great fireworks displays, probably the most ambitious pyrotechnic exhibitions anywhere in the world, were resumed and, because of the elevated position of the Palace, gave delight to the whole of London, from where they were visible once weekly during summer. Among other things, the Battle of Jutland was a favourite spectacle with the crowds. This was staged on the north lake where model ships and fireworks combined to produce the greatest sea fight of all history. In view of the enormous amount of explosive substance required, and the fact that many of the displays called for the use of stunt men covered in fireworks and protected by asbestos suits, great tribute is due to the organisers for the fact that throughout the years not one case of accident or injury was ever reported at the Crystal Palace fireworks displays.

Before concluding this summary of the period of restoration, mention must be made of John Logie Baird the inventor of television. He approached and was granted by Henry Buckland certain facilities for experiment and production at the Palace, which included parts of the south transept basement, and the south tower. Later, the south wing and colonnade were to become Baird's main centre of production. In a nation where it would be difficult to find a home without television, it is amazing how few are those who know that the Crystal Palace was the birthplace of their main source of entertainment, news, and to some extent education and enlightenment.

In the spring of 1931, Henry Buckland was created a Knight by King George V. As Sir Henry Buckland he had won his country's gratitude for saving and restoring the Crystal Palace. Since the fire of 1936, certain writers and, more recently, television producers have convoyed the impression that during its last few years the Crystal Palace was, for the most part, derelict. At its worst, this is a downright untruth. At its best, it is a pathetic attempt to perpetuate a legend fostered by those who would like us to believe that the loss of the Palace was of no great concern to anyone. On the personal plane, it was a cruel source of hurt to Sir Henry Buckland's surviving family, who I know from close contact, aware of just how hard he worked and strove to make his beloved Palace live as Sir Joseph Paxton would have wished. Like all humans, Sir Henry Buckland was imperfect in many respects. Some of his imperfections were a built-in part of his nature, some can be directly related to the times in which he lived; times which were far from easy and only understood by those who lived through them. Of his many years at the Crystal Palace in his capacity as General Manager, it can be said in all truth that here was a man devoted to his task which, in the face of enormous impediment and obstacle, he performed with undoubted success. During the 1920s and 1930s, a sum of money running to six figures was spent solely on restoration and general improvement. In 1936, the only serious deficiency in the Crystal Palace lay in the realm of internal fire prevention and containment.

Chapter four

Brigade call

The year of 1936 was troubled indeed. The year had but dawned when on January 21st King George V died, leaving behind him a grieving nation. For he was much-loved, having along with his Consort Queen Mary, done more than any previous crowned head to bring the monarchy forward and into line with modern thought. On the last day of November, the Crystal Palace was destroyed and eighty-four years of tradition upholding all that was best of the Victorian era went with it. December was to see Great Britain plunged into the worst con-stitutional crisis in all the nation's long history. The crisis was brought about by King Edward VIII and his love for a commoner, and divorcee, culminating in his abdication.

For the most part, the remainder of this book will concern itself with the great fire which was the eclipse of the Crystal Palace as it was known and loved by millions of people at that time. In order to avoid confusion, this chapter will be confined to a description of the fire, and the action taken by the fire brigades in fighting it. Part five, however, will be concerned with a searching investigation of the possible causes, and the strange and far from normal circumstances related to the fire which have come to light as a result of four years' probing by the writer; probing which has required the painstaking tracking down and careful questioning of witnesses; many of whom were found to have died or moved on. A most essential requirement to this investigation has been the study of a mass of paperwork consisting of documents, press reports and many letters from various people who have kindly responded to the writer's repeated requests for assistance.

For the layman, and for those not familiar with fire brigade organisation as it existed prior to the Second World War, it must be pointed out that, unlike today, there was no nationwide concept of an integrated fire service, organised on standardised equipment and operational procedure, with standard training and operational technique laid down by a Home Office committee of experts, in concert with qualified fire engineers. What we did have was a multiplicity of independent fire brigades each belonging to its own particular city and town, and controlled by its own chief officer who was responsible for purchasing equipment right down the line, from major mobile appliances to his men's uniforms and cap badges. The choice, and hence the suitability of this equipment, depended on two yardsticks – the particular whim of the chief officer, and the amount of money which he was able to prise from his city or town administration; some were generous, some were reluctant to make money available for what they saw as necessary evils, like fire brigades and ambulance services.

Strange as it may seem to us today, there were several instances up and down the country of what were known as 'Police Fire Brigades'. This was a wholly ludicrous exercise in meanness and penny-pinching where police and fire brigade was one service, men working as policemen one week and firemen the next, on a rota basis. This system held sway in several towns and cities, and the fact that it worked at all was due only to the great sense of devotion and public spiritedness of those unfortunate enough to have to make it work. Wholly combined fire ambulance brigades were commonplace, but not as bad in concept because some similarity does exist between the two; in the Police Fire Brigade there is none.

Between one locality and another, equipment differed considerably and so did methods. It required the Second World War and the fire blitz to expose the deadly weakness of a system where even hose couplings which worked in one city were quite useless in another because sizes varied; some were instantaneous, some threaded. Operational orders and signals by means of hand semaphore, where noisy conditions made oral instructions unreliable, differed too, with the result that reinforcements sent from one part of the country to another faced meaningless orders and signals.

Of the equipment itself, it must be admitted that most of it was good and well looked after, manufacturers of firefighting equipment generally maintaining meticulous standards and refusing cut-price tenders. The brigades themselves much prided in keeping their engines well turned out. Because of the great diversity of organisation, methods and equipment, efficiency was bound to vary and difficult to measure, there being no set yardstick, and much argument and debate as to the merits of four very large fire brigades; London, Paris, New York and Chicago. When looked at rationally, it was a fruitless argument for the reason that all four locations are as different as chalk and cheese. This is especially so when comparing Paris and London with the two American cities, which have very different layouts, and very different building construction. However all that may be, because of its position as the centre of a great empire and seat of government, because of its huge population and importance as a tourist attraction, because of its vast wealth in property and historic treasure London has, since the early nineteenth century, possessed a fire brigade second to none and dating back to the day when James Braidwood, a Scot from Edinburgh, came south to become superintendent of the London Fire Engine Establishment. Braidwood laid the foundations well but, unfortunately, before his task was completed, he was killed by a falling wall at the disastrous Tooley Street fire of 1861. His successor Eyre Massey Shaw an Irishman from Dublin, and of Scots-Irish parents, was to continue the work of Braidwood by improving, extending and enhancing what had already been done. Shaw's greatest personal gratification, apart from his knighthood, was probably to see the London Fire Engine Establishment removed from the hands of the insurance companies to become a publicly-owned utility on 1st January 1866, when The Metropolitan Fire Brigade was established. Under Massey Shaw's genius, and the guiding hand of a succession of what, for the most part, have proven to be well-chosen chief officers, the Metropolitan Fire Brigade, later renamed the London Fire Brigade had, by the 1930s, become the envy of the world.

A state of inefficiency tends to spread outwards from its centre, infecting and fouling up that which lies on its fringe. A state of high efficiency works in the same direction infecting what lies on its fringe with its own enthusiasm and drive for perfection. So it came about, that the smaller independent fire brigades responsible for the areas bordering London were as good as London's own brigade. Only in numbers of men and appliances were they at a disadvantage, and this was unavoidable because their areas of responsibility were much smaller. Before 1936, a move was already in hand to go some way in the direction of overcoming this particular problem. Luckily for the country as a whole, there were, during the 'thirties some far-sighted men both in London's fire brigade headquarters and in brigade headquarters in other cities and towns.

Arrangements were being made for the London Fire Brigade to respond to a call for assistance from outside its own borders in exceptionally serious circumstances. In this way, the first tentative steps had been taken along the road toward a nationally orientated fire service although, so far as London was concerned, the possibility of movement to areas beyond the Capital had been recognised as far back as 1865 when the Metropolitan Fire Brigades Act had been drawn up (but more of that later, for the Act had within it a serious flaw which hindered rather than helped mobility beyond the county border).

It was decided that if the Crystal Palace were ever to catch fire, it would represent an exceptionally serious circumstance calling for the assistance of the London Fire Brigade. Arrangements were implemented with the brigades in the Crystal Palace area whereby they could call upon London if the need should arise, regardless of the aforementioned Act. As excellent an arrangement as this was, it contained a further flaw, which the various fire brigades were aware of but unable to remedy, and which is appropriate of discussion here. The London Fire Brigade had, for many years, been armed with a Bye-Law which gave it right of access to, and the power to insist upon certain rigid fire prevention and fire containment measures being provided for, as specified by brigade experts in all theatres, cinemas, and exhibition halls within the London county.

Long before 1936, the London Fire Brigade had found reason to become seriously concerned about the Crystal Palace for what they viewed as a generally unsatisfactory state of fire precautions there, in respect of the huge number of people which could be accommodated within the building at any one time. This concern was engendered by a proposal for all the London schools to hold a great concert at the Palace in 1932, and the Brigade made a written approach to the Crystal Palace management requesting permission to inspect the building, and offering advice with a view to improving things.

For reasons which will become apparent later, the approach fell on deaf ears, and there was nothing to be done about it, because the Brigade's powers stopped short at the London county border, which ran through the gateway to the Palace on Crystal Palace Parade, the building itself remaining just beyond reach in Kent County.

The London schools plan for a great concert at Crystal Palace was cancelled because of the lack of co-operation on the part of the Crystal Palace management and, in view of this, the London Fire Brigade had only one option open to them – to advise the County Education Authority that they were unable to accept responsibility for the children's safety in the event of fire. Because of this lack of co-operation, any attempt at a prearranged plan for dealing with an outbreak of fire at the Palace was thwarted by refusal of access, both for a really accurate appraisal of conditions within the building and on the site exercises with appliances, which is the only way of discovering snags, condition and location of alternative water supplies, and the best positions for placing men and equipment. True, to some extent this could be done by means of large-scale maps, building plans and models; those devices however are no match for on the spot inspections, exercises, and drills. Nevertheless, the London Fire Brigade stuck fast to its original plan to come to the assistance of the local brigades if asked to, complemented by an amendment, namely the informative procedure which requested that they be informed of any outbreak at the Palace, even if it was found to be within the resources of the local brigades to cope without assistance.

....

The evening of Monday 30th November 1936 was fine, with little cloud. The wind was moderate to strong and holding steady from the northwest. Aircraft were operating normally in and out of Croydon Airport only a few miles from Sydenham. The temperature was cold but without frost.

At 7:59pm, a call was received at Penge Fire Station, in Croydon Road, Penge, reporting a fire at the Crystal Palace. It is doubtful if we will ever know for certain from where and from whom this call originated. The same applies with Beckenham Fire Brigade who were in receipt of a similar call just over a minute later. The duty firemen acting as watch room attendants and who actually handled the calls cannot remember the origins. As for the time, there is no shadow of doubt, for it is well corroborated. The reader would be advised to bear in mind that moment in time – 7:59pm; repeated reference will be made to it, for upon it a great deal hangs.

Penge Fire Brigade, in whose area most of the Crystal Palace lay, responded at once with their full strength of one motor pump and eight men in the charge of Chief Officer J. Goodman. An uphill journey of under four minutes brought them to Crystal Palace Parade where they were at once confronted by an alarming and totally unexpected sight. Alarming, because the entire centre transept of the Palace was engulfed in flames from end to end, and from ground level to the uppermost point of the great arched vault. Totally unexpected because, on several previous occasions, Penge firemen had been called to the Palace for minor reasons of rubbish and dry grass burning in the grounds; and because the unknown person who called Penge brigade gave no indication whatsoever of the extent or the seriousness of the situation, as it must have been, and indeed, has proved to have been, less than four minutes earlier before mounting his appliance. Chief Officer Goodman instructed his watch room attendant to send off a message to London Fire Brigade Headquarters informing them to put London on a red alert if it should be required.

While the Penge motor pump was getting to work from a hydrant a little north of the centre transept, the two Beckenham motor pumps arrived, connecting to hydrants opposite the south transept. Having realised at once that the Palace was already far beyond the help of his very limited resources, and while his men were getting to work, Chief Officer Goodman called the London Fire Brigade by exchange telephone asking for direct assistance; the time now being 8:05pm. As it transpired, assistance was already well on its way. At 8:00pm someone in West Norwood, alarmed by the glow in the sky over Sydenham and having the Palace in mind, called the West Norwood station of the London Fire Brigade. This call was followed almost simultaneously by further calls both by street fire alarm and exchange telephone. Deciding that so many calls could only indicate a serious fire, the Chief Officer at West Norwood informed the London Fire Brigade.

Headquarters on the Albert Embankment asking for a District Call to be sent out alerting all stations southeast of the Thames. The Chief Officer of the London Fire Brigade at the time was the late Major C. C. B. Morris, C.B.E., M.C., M. I. Mech. E. In his autobiography, (Fire! Published by Blackie, 1939) Major Morris relates how he was just finishing dinner when at 8:00pm the telephone rang in his flat to inform him of a district call to the Crystal Palace. Major Morris continues with the following: 'From the balcony at the back of my flat on the fourth floor of our new Headquarters, I could see the Palace quite clearly in daytime, and on stepping outside hurriedly to try to see if there was any sign of a fire, I saw a dull red glow lighting up the whole of the centre transept. Definitely a late call – the fire must have been going at least half an hour before we received our first call – we shall probably lose the whole building.' In due course we shall discover that Major Morris was making an under-statement when he wrote of half an hour. In fact, the time lapse was considerably in excess of half an hour, although he could not possibly have known it at the time. Being a man of undoubted honesty any statement made by Major Morris is a statement of fact as it existed, and is therefore of prime value when we come to evaluate evidence.

It took about thirty seconds for Major Morris to change into his fire kit and be on his way in the brigade staff car, accompanied by his two assistants, Chief Commander A. N. G. Firebrace, and Major T. W. Jackson. Appliances from Headquarters preceded the staff car, having left within fifteen seconds from receipt of the first call. As the staff car was swinging out onto the Albert Embankment, Major Morris was informed that a Brigade Call had just come in.

At this juncture it is appropriate to explain that a District Call indicates a serious fire requiring the response of all stations within the district, in this case south and southeast London. A Brigade Call is the ultimate, indicating a major conflagration calling for the response of every station within the capital. By 8:05pm therefore, 'the bells had gone down' at every fire station in London, and the streets were reverberating from the sound of fire bells as men and machines converged on Sydenham from all parts. This must have been something of a sight when one remembers that in those days most fire appliances were of the open type with the Braidwood body construction, the men in highly polished brass helmets either sitting precariously or hanging on for grim death to any hand-hold within reach on their swaying, fast-accelerating, swerving red monsters as they wove their way through city traffic. Many will say that the modern all-enclosed fire appliance with its wailing two-tone siren has nothing of the glamour and excitement of the old, open bell-ringing machines. One must always allow for sentiment, but the fact is that the old fire bell has been proved to be inaudible in conditions of modern city traffic, and in bad weather the open type body was dangerous not only because of the very real risk of men losing their grip and falling, or rather being thrown off, but also because their chances of catching pneumonia from their being exposed to the weather were a near certainty at some point of their career. In fact, among firemen the open appliance was often referred to as 'the pneumonia wagon'.

Meanwhile, at the Palace the situation was worsening with frightening rapidity. Within a few minutes of the arrival of the Penge, Beckenham, and Croydon brigades, the entire front of the great centre transept fell outwards on to Crystal Palace Parade, and at 8:10pm the whole massive transept collapsed in a mighty shower of sparks and a terrible roar which was heard several miles distant. The fire now spread north and south into the naves, its worst ferocity being concentrated on the south nave, the northerly wind blowing the flames and furnace-like heat in that direction. Prior to the fall of the centre transept, men of the Penge brigade had forced an entry to the north nave in an attempt to contain the fire within the centre transept. Backed by reinforcements arriving from London, a similar tactic was mounted in the south nave, some success being evident at both locations until the fall of the transept, when flames of great length began running into both naves high up in the arched vault under the roof, and out of reach of the firemen's jets. The immediate result of this was a hail of molten lead, aluminium and glass falling on the heads of the men, rendering their position suicidal and thus forcing their withdrawal and an end, at least for the time being, to further operations from inside the building.

Almost from the outset, and most certainly before the collapse of the centre transept, two factors were adversely affecting the efforts and impairing the efficiency of the firefighters. The first, and in the long run the most serious, was shortage of water. This inadequacy was demonstrated dramatically upon the arrival of one of the earliest reinforcements. Croydon Fire Brigade had one motor pump, one turntable ladder fitted with its own pump, and eleven men with Chief Officer P. W. Delve in charge. In an attempt to control the fire in the centre transept, the turntable ladder was 'shot up' to its full length of 100ft, far short of the ideal height. This is accepted as being one where the head of the ladder projects some distance above the burning roof, so that the powerful monitor-controlled jet of water can be aimed downwards and sideways to the best advantage, as seen by the fireman directing the monitor from his commanding position at the head of the ladder. This was a serious impediment, but far worse was the pathetic trickle of water which came from the monitor, and which defied improvement because the pumps in action were draughting the mains dry. In a letter to this writer, Officer Delve, now Sir Frederick Delve C.B.E. and an ex-Chief Officer of the London Fire Brigade, retired in 1962, stated that 'The water supplies in the mains for firefighting were totally inadequate in volume to deal with a fire of this magnitude'.

The second adverse factor was the vast crowd of onlookers who, from the beginning, began jamming Crystal Palace Parade and its approaches on foot, on bicycles and in motor cars, impeding the free movement of fire-fighting equipment and men to such an extent that many appliances were held up for so long that they were of little use when, finally, they did get through. So dense and so uncontrolled did this seething mass of humanity become that in the end 3,000 policemen were required to drive them back and cordon off the area.

The appearance of so many onlookers is easily explained. The Crystal Palace, because of its elevated position, was visible from all over London; it followed therefore that once alight it represented a beacon, a huge bonfire visible for a considerable distance, and bound to attract the interest of all who could see it, as well as those who only heard of it by way of what has been considered by some to be a premature news broadcast made in thoughtless haste by BBC radio. It is difficult, in light of advanced experience with radio communications, to decide whether or not criticism of the BBC is valid in this instance.

Such then was the unenviable situation awaiting Major Morris and his colleagues upon their assuming command, shortly before the collapse of the great centre transept. A fast-dwindling supply of water and a vast, uncontrolled crowd getting in the way of, and seriously hindering the firemen and, as things worsened, exposing them to increasing danger. Some were even hostile towards the firemen, blaming them for a late arrival and their apparent inability to stop the fire spreading. Not knowing about the late call and the practical difficulties facing the fire brigades, their attitude is perhaps excusable but was, nonetheless, a menace at the time, and one with which the police were forced to deal quickly and efficiently.

When the tides of fortune turn against men they never do so singularly. Shortage of water, uncontrolled crowds of humanity milling about and getting in the way, the northerly wind increasing in strength, and a further devil lurking inside the burning Palace, as yet unseen and unrealised – gas – which had not been turned off although, in due course, there would be evidence to suggest a belated and not very resolute attempt to do so.

The collapse of the centre transept at 8:10pm should, in theory at least, have helped matters. A fire in an environment once out of control and burning freely builds up heat at a speed hard to appreciate if one has never experienced it. If this rapid rise in temperature cannot be halted and reduced by one means or another, a point is reached at which a phenomenon occurs known as 'flash over'. This is a state in which materials of a combustible nature have become heated to a temperature at which they will commence to burn and flash into flame of their own accord, thus spreading fire in every direction with explosive force.

One very successful method of reducing a rise in temperature leading to a state of 'flash over' is to vent the heat upwards and outwards through the roof of the burning building. This can be done in three ways. Skylights glazed with one of several synthetic substances designed to fail at a predetermined temperature can be built into the roof. Known as automatic venting, this method is in wide use today, and is responsible for many structures surviving fires which without it would have destroyed them. In the absence of automatic venting, a similar result can be achieved manually by opening up the roof with forced entry tools. Thirdly, a partial, or total collapse of the roof will bring about a rapid, although somewhat belated venting of heat and smoke, at once reducing the temperature dramatically. It would, therefore, be reasonable to expect that when the roof of the centre transept fell, in the fierce heat contained within, the structure would vent itself safely to the sky where it could do no harm. Had such normality have existed at the Crystal Palace, the firemen would have gained a few minutes of immensely valuable time in which to beat down the remaining fire and stop any serious spread into the main building, i.e. the north and south naves.

Unfortunately there was no normality at the Crystal Palace. Apart from the difficulties already referred to, the building itself was abnormal in as much as its construction was almost unique. Unlike structures of stone, brick, or concrete, this fabric of delicate glass and spidery ironwork disintegrated at a speed far in excess of the contents. Thus, when the centre transept had ceased to exist as an integrated structure and had become instead a fallen ruin of twisted iron and molten glass, its enormous content of flimsy timber staging, seating, and highly combustible organ was just getting stoked up to its full efficiency of heat-producing blast. When the transept collapsed, the blistering heat from the conflagration inside was too much to vent upwards completely, leaving much of it to disperse sideways into the naves which had already become heated dangerously close to 'flash over'. The flames high up under the roof which had driven the firemen out a few minutes earlier, became transformed in a matter of seconds into something resembling a giant's blowtorch, causing the naves to glow and flame. The northerly wind leaping into the vortex left by the doomed transept increased the blowtorch ferocity of fire and heat in the south nave, until the effect was similar to forced draught in the grate of a high-pressure boiler. On the north side, this effect was nothing like so pronounced. Because of the wind pushing the fire in the opposite direction and the barrier protection afforded by the solid stonework of the Period Courts the north nave was, for a short time, spared and intact, and was to some extent to survive the worst of the catastrophe.

A situation with all the ingredients of first-degree disaster was now materialising. The fire in the south nave, fanned by wind and feeding on escaping gas, was beginning to involve the south transept, and close to this, indeed much too close for any comfort, was the looming bulk of the giant 293ft high south tower overlooking the heavily populated Anerley Hill, which was packed almost solid with thousands of spectators, many of whom had overflowed into the gardens of houses. Some of the more athletic were even up in the treetops, atop lamp standards and on the roofs of houses, all oblivious to the danger fast bearing down upon them, caring only for a better view.

Deep under the Palace, another of those devils had flexed its muscles after awakening from a sleep which had lasted unbroken since the day when Sir Joseph Paxton had, in all innocence, included it in his scheme of things. Now joining forces with those of its kin already at work, it was helping to destroy the nave and transept, while at the same time commencing an underground assault on the south tower. This latest manifestation of evil was the basement area where, it will be recalled, the central heating boilers had their domain. Having from the beginning found its way into the basement, the fire was soon roaring through, igniting the main timber floor of the building above, and finding its way upwards into the Palace through the pipe ducts and the metal grilles of the heating system to unite with the giant's blowtorch raging through the first floor. The savagery of the fire within the Paxton Tunnel and basement was sufficient to crack and to melt the flue pipes connecting with the vertical chimney-casing enclosed within the south tower, so that the fire was actually being drawn into the tower, albeit contained within the chimney casing; here it remained confined. The only outward evidence of this was an ugly plume of acrid smoke streaming away on the wind from the shallow stack outlet on the tower's summit. It was this plume of smoke which gave rise to the rumour that the tower itself was burning. In fact it never was more than a rumour, but it gave birth to a story much publicised in the newspapers of the next day – that the south tower was on fire – and hence to a legend ever since.

It would seem, on available evidence, that the fire brigades were never aware of the threat from the Paxton Tunnel or basement, otherwise orders to flood them would doubtless have been given. For this oversight the fire brigades were blameless, for they were the victims of a system which had resolutely denied them a chance of ever becoming familiar with the interior layout of this gigantic complex. This lack of detailed knowledge proved throughout to be the ultimate frustration and the worst single opponent in a battle which was lost before it started; a battle which nevertheless was to continue being fought for many hours with outstanding courage and bravery.

At 9:00pm the situation was at its most frightening from the point of view of mere spectacle, and most dangerous in the practical sense. There was, by this time, an unbroken front of uncontrolled fire extending for close on half a mile with a width, or depth, of nearly 403ft, and throwing flames over 300ft into the night sky. The ferocious updraught of heat was carrying sparks and even blazing brands of debris high into the air and, assisted by the wind, was depositing them over a wide area, some falling at Beckenham two miles distant. The lurid glow in the sky was to be seen from places as far apart as Brighton, Southend-on-Sea, Margate, and St. Albans. Two airline pilots, one Captain J. T. Percy of Imperial Airways and another, Captain Van Weyrother of KLM Royal Dutch Airlines, reported seeing the blaze from fifty miles away over the English Channel.

According to both pilots, the clouds over southeast England appeared blood red, and on the terrace of the House of Commons many members were to be seen watching the flickering glare to the southeast.

On the fire ground, the dwindling water supply had come to the point of desperation, and at 9:00pm it was impossible, without a vacuum reading showing on the gauge, to obtain water for four ¾-inch jets from one of the Beckenham pumps; and this grim picture was repeating itself at every point where an appliance was working. The initial shortage of water had deteriorated to a state where there was no water of any consequence; through a lack of co-ordination between the several brigades, and even between units of the same brigade, a situation had arisen where everyone was grabbing for everything, and ending up with nothing.

In order to achieve some measure of coordination, a central control position was set up in the relative safety of the High Level Railway Station booking office, and placed in the charge of the late Mr. F. Dann, who in later years was to gain high rank in the fire service. Much respected, and loved by colleagues and friends alike, it was with regret that this writer received news of Mr. Dann's death, just prior to an interview requested by the writer.

From Frank Dann's makeshift control room a desperately urgent call went out to the Metropolitan Water Board for an increase in pressure. To provide this, non-essential supplies were cut off over a wide area and an immediate improvement was apparent. But it was still nothing like what was required and it was obvious, in view of the mounting danger to the south tower, that recourse to other supplies would have to be made.

The end of the south transept had collapsed, having been pushed outwards by the super-heated expanded air inside, and a tornado of flame was swirling through the entire length of the nave and transept destroying all in its path. Osler's Crystal Fountain was reduced to molten glass. The carved wood and bronze screen with all its Kings and Queens was gone along with the Great Clock, and the hundreds of pieces of statuary in this part of the building. As the great arched roof began to twist in torment, sag, and then crash to earth amid showers of white-hot debris, so the flames began to race through the wooden outbuildings towards the base of the south tower. In order to make more water available in the mains at the building's southern extremity, all jets along Crystal Palace Parade were ordered to be shut down. It was now no longer practical to save the main structure except for the north transept. There was little left but liquid glass and white hot iron, and the last drop of water which the pumps could squeeze from the mains looked like being insufficient to prevent the south tower from crashing onto the houses bordering Anerley Hill.

Only a week previously the London Fire Brigade had acquired a new machine. This was a hose-laying unit which could run out twin lines of hose at speeds up to 30mph. The huge machine was rushed to the lake at the north end of the Palace, and set to work laying down hose along the terrace on the garden front, this route being more direct and much less congested than the Palace Parade. All went well for some distance until, because of the soft gravel surface now soaked with water, the new unit became bogged down and unable to move. Being such a very heavy vehicle designed for use on firm roads it was just too much for the soft, spongy terrace, so the hoses were manhandled the rest of the way to the south tower where a water relay was set up.

At the Crystal Palace, recourse to the upper lake was something of a gamble. The hose-laying appliance was new, the men unfamiliar with it, and the relay itself something of a leap in the dark. It speaks highly for the firemen's ability to improvise quickly when, after some short-lived difficulties requiring adjustment, the men at the south tower began receiving sufficient water to direct a barrage of heavy jets on the fire now roaring through the wooden outbuildings with the speed of a dry brush fire. The relay was working so well that the fire was finally stopped 15ft from the base of the tower and the barrage of heavy jets, besides causing the fire to retreat, was also flooding the basement and Paxton Tunnel, drowning the fire there.

At about this time, several explosions shook the ruins of the south transept. It is not known if these explosions were caused by pockets of gas which were still coursing freely through the mains and escaping where these were broken, or by bursting bottles of industrial gas, many of these being used by the Baird Television Company for various processes connected with its work. Whether or not the explosions had been triggered by town gas, if firemen were to penetrate the glowing remains of the Palace, the poisonous fumes had to be eliminated. The normal cut-off valves had become inaccessible, and distorted so as to be useless, so at about 9:15pm the gas authority started digging up the road outside the centre transept and, after searching for about half an hour, unearthed the gas main feeding the Palace about 1ft 6in to 2ft beneath the road. This they cut and sealed, using a bladder for the purpose of making tight the live end. The pressure on this could not have been greater than about $\frac{1}{2}$lbf/in2, i.e. normal low-pressure district mains, otherwise use of a bladder would not be possible. Town gas was now cut off from the whole complex, and the firemen were enabled to move in without fear of explosion or gas poisoning.

The saving of the south tower marked the turn of tide for the hard-pressed firemen, and the negation of grim possibilities. Had the tower fallen on the congested Anerley Hill the resulting carnage is easy to imagine. The firemen's troubles were not over, however. At about 9:30pm the wind backed sharply to the west, followed quickly by a further movement to a point approximately west by southwest. The result of this change of wind was to blow the fire into the north nave, as yet not seriously involved, at least when compared with what had happened to the rest of the building. Up to now the firemen, because of the lack of water, had been able to carry out a holding operation, but not much else, on the northern end of the structure. Now that the south tower was out of danger and water more plentiful, men were ordered into the north nave with instructions to use their jets against the fire now spreading rapidly on the southerly wind, only to face a repetition of what had defeated them in the south nave where, as previously described, flames of great length started running the roof, showering the men with a hail of molten glass and metal, forcing their retreat.

Concern for the safety of the north tower was now uppermost for the fire chiefs. Although the tower was some distance from the main building, a collection of gardeners' huts and greenhouses filled much of the intervening space and there were signs of fire spreading through

40

them. Fortunately the upper lake, with its 6,500,000 gallons of water, was close at hand. Pumps were set into the lake and coupled up to deluge sets, sometimes referred to as monitors or water cannon, which can project streams of enormous volume through nozzles of four-inch diameter capable of smashing right through the walls of the average dwelling house. Once in action, the fire in the north nave was quickly subdued by the weight and volume of water rushing from the deluge sets; hand-controlled jets easily extinguished the burning greenhouses and gardeners' huts. To supplement the ground attack, four turntable ladders positioned on Crystal Palace Parade were pouring thousands of gallons of water onto the roof of the nave and these, combined with the ground attack, all copiously supplied from the lake soon had the fire overwhelmed. Although most of the glass had gone, the iron framework remained standing and at 11:45pm Major Morris circulated the 'Stop Message', indicating that the fire was under control and no further assistance required.

Some idea of the quantity of water used on the north nave can be gauged from the fact that eleven pumps, each with a capacity of one thousand gallons per minute, were drawing from the lake; eleven thousand gallons per minute in all. Had such a volume been on hand at the outset the Palace would, in all probability, have been saved.

As the deluge sets were shut down, firemen with hand jets advanced into the ruined nave. The scene of desolation which confronted them was terrible to behold. For the most part the timber floor had burned away leaving a red-hot gridiron of twisted metal, congealed glass, and charred beams. Much of the Period Courts had survived, but the damage sustained by them was shocking; on every hand were the pathetic remains of decapitated statues standing forlorn amidst broken pillars, overlooked by scorched and blackened carvings, friezes and murals. One of the world's finest art collections, and a structure unique in the annals of architecture was now reduced, in a matter of four hours, to a grotesque, hideous nightmare, representing a criminal desecration brought about by neglect on the part of those who had the power to have provided money, which if properly spent could have rendered the Palace safe and secure for posterity.

The centre transept, the south nave and transept were reduced to a glowing residue in which nothing of consequence remained, and yet the fish in the basins of the Bronze and Crystal Fountains were found to be alive, still swimming and apparently none the worse for their experience, except that their scales had changed colour from gold to black. The many tropical birds had been released from their cages soon after the fire started and, fluttering through the heat and smoke, had found their way out, seeking refuge in nearby trees.

The Baird Television Company lost ninety per cent of its experimental equipment located in the south transept basement, but the receiving sets production department, in the south wing on Anerley Hill, was not damaged.

Throughout the night and the next day, firemen cooled down debris and dealt with small outbreaks. At 5:00pm it was possible for the last of the London Fire Brigade units to leave, and Superintendent C. I. Wright left the smoking ruins in charge of Chief Goodman of Penge, whose men were to spend the rest of the week turning over and damping down the wreckage. There was no loss of life and little injury. Four firemen were hurt by burns and cuts; they were firemen S. R. Stenton, E. E. Crutch, E. A. Freeborn, and Station Officer Cox. This was a miracle, considering that the fire was the biggest in the London Fire Brigade's history to that date. The total attendance was 88 appliances and 438 officers and men, including three units and twenty-three personnel of the London Salvage Corps. The previous record was the Colonial Wharf, Wapping rubber fire on 25th September 1935. This called for 82 appliances and 360 men.

The make-up of appliances and men for the Crystal Palace fire was:

Fire Brigade Headquarters	Major C.C.B. Morris, M.C.	In overall command
	Commander A.N.G. Firebrace	
	Major F.W. Jackson, D.S.O.	
	C. M. Kerr J. H. Fordham	Assistant Divisional Officers
	C. J. Wright	Superintendent
	L. A. Shearman	District Officer
London Fire Brigade		
8 Dual-purpose Machines, 53 Pumps, 4 Turntable Ladders, 12 Cars, 2 Fire Lorries. 7 Lorries & 2 Emergency Tenders, 1 Canteen Van, 381 officers & men		
Penge Brigade	J. Goodman	Chief Officer
Motor Combination, 7 men & Supt. 2 Motor pumps, 1 Motor Tender, 11 men		
Beckenham Brigade	J. H. P. Evans	Chief Officer
2 Motor Pumps, 1 Tender, & 11 men	Mr. Jameson	Deputy Chief Officer
Croydon Brigade	F. W. Delve	Chief Officer
2 Motor Appliances, 2 Cars, 8 men & 11 men		
London Salvage Corps	G. H. Whiteman	Chief Officer
3 Salvage Tenders, 1 motor car & 21 men	Supt. W. J. Blyth	

The Croydon turntable ladder which attended the Crystal Palace fire, a Leyland-Metz, first registered on 27th April 1936, with the registration number AVB1 and retired from service in 1968, is now in the care of Fire Brigades of Surrey Preservation Trust, at Surrey Fire and Rescue Service Headquarters, Croydon Road, Reigate, Surrey, RH2 0EJ, beautifully restored.

For several days following the fire, thousands of sightseers caused heavy congestion in the area, and for a time the police ordered a one-way traffic movement along Crystal Palace Parade. During the afternoon of 1st December, H. M. Queen Mary paid her last respects to the Palace by driving slowly along the Parade. She did not stop, but her face registered her sorrow as she glanced at the smoking ruins of an institution known to have been dear both to herself and to her late husband King George V.

Almost every newspaper in the land gave front page coverage to the fire, which was recognised to be a national disaster without equal in its time. Newspapers and radio stations in many parts of the world echoed the heartbreaking news, and Sir Henry Buckland was inundated with messages of sympathy and offers of help. His immediate problems were multiplied because 1937 was to be Coronation year, and the Palace was more heavily booked than at any time in its history; alternative arrangements had to be put in hand at once.

As the immediate shock of the disaster receded, so rumour and speculation about the cause of the fire mounted; the words sabotage and arson began to raise their ugly meanings in the public mind. How could a building of glass and iron burn? That was the question perplexing many, with the result that Sydenham and its environs became the centre for suspicion and, ultimately, for lurid stories involving Sir Henry Buckland himself who, for reasons both obvious and obscure, was much disliked by many. As this writer was to discover, this suspicion and dislike persist to this day, long after Sir Henry Buckland has passed on, presenting a fog so dense as to create a baffling mystery which often seemed to be impossible of penetration or solution.

Major Morris wrote further in his memoirs: 'by the morning the building was a forlorn, menacing wreck. 100,000 panes of shattered glass hampered salvage work and 15,000 tons of twisted iron girders and framework solidified gradually from the molten metal into grotesque shapes and rivers of frozen steel. In these halls of havoc girders, planks, turnstiles and cast-iron fittings are strewn in a tangled, distorted mass'.

Chapter five

Accident or Arson?

'Why did it burn like it did?…it was made of glass and iron.' Such was the question and the observation on millions of lips on the morning of December 1st 1936. The inference, of course, is obvious. Because the Crystal Palace was constructed of iron and glass, the public for the most part believed it to be fireproof; an unfounded belief providing fertile soil in which theories of arson would flourish, ensuring that the idea of a simple accident would wither and die.

The Crystal Palace did not burn in the accepted sense of burning. The iron and the glass did not catch fire, but they did distort and melt, with total collapse of the structure as an inevitable result. The distortion of the iron framework and the melting of the glass fabric were induced by heat generated by the burning of highly combustible interior fittings and appointments.

The truly fireproof structure is for the most part a myth existing, if at all, in the form of a monument fashioned from solid incombustibles, e.g. stone, concrete, iron, steel, bronze, or in the form of the burial chamber or tomb. Nelson's Column, the Victoria Memorial and the tomb of Tutankhamen, can all be said to be fireproof.

Had the Crystal Palace been erected purely in glass and iron, remaining empty of any kind of furnishing, unheated, and without illumination, then it would probably have been immune from fire, but totally useless in any practical sense.

Having disposed of the myth of a fireproof Crystal Palace, we are left with a problem. How did its contents catch fire and burn with such rapidity as to defy every effort to save a building which had survived three previous fires, two of them serious?

....

'A Streak of flame ran along the top of the room and the place was ablaze in a moment. The time was 7:25pm. I thought at first that gas was the cause; now we know.' Thus pronounced Sir Henry Buckland on the morning after the fire when questioned by the press in his capacity as General Manager and custodian of the Crystal Palace.

During the course of the next few days, Sir Henry Buckland was to make other statements, some of them conflicting and contradictory, concerning his movements and his actions during the early stages of the fire, but never at any time did he deviate from his theory about gas being the cause; a theory which he stuck to, and carried with him to the grave. A theory which in one respect, and at one point, was to develop into the realm of fantasy, and from which he was never forced to retract.

Retraction was not forced upon him because, although the smoking ruins were combed the following day by official-looking men in bowler hats, and others with cameras, these men were in fact only insurance loss assessors and London Fire Brigade photographers compiling a pictorial record for the Brigade's historical library.

There was no inquiry because there was no fatal accident. In a letter to Sir Edward Campbell, M.P., who had raised the matter and asked for an inquiry in the Commons, Mr. Geoffrey Lloyd, then Parliamentary Under Secretary of State for the Home Department, said that the Home Secretary had no power to hold an inquiry into the Crystal Palace fire, because there was no power, except in the City of London under a special Act, to hold a Fire 'inquest' in cases where no fatalities had occurred.

Mr. Geoffrey Lloyd's letter was dated 14th December 1936 and, in spite of Sir Edward Campbell's obvious misgivings leading him to deduce that something was not as it should be, that letter was to kill stone dead any further initiative along those lines. So Sir Henry Buckland was left in comparative peace to firmly maintain that gas was the scapegoat, and on the 1st December 1936, he made the following statement to the press: 'When I got to the office I found two of the three night-duty firemen already at work with a hose. They did all they could, but the fire was very close to a big gas container. I cannot but think that the gas must have ignited early.'

There was no gas container big or small near the fire, or anywhere else in the building except for the south transept basement, where there were a number of industrial welding bottles used by Baird Television in its day-to-day manufacturing process. None of those bottles was big, or a container of gas in the meaning of Sir Henry Buckland's words. On examination of the wrecked building the nearest gas bottle was found to have been a quarter of a mile from the fire's location in its early stages, and nothing remotely resembling an industrial gas bottle was found anywhere near the area of initial outbreak. Even so, this particular mare's nest seemed at one point to have at least a smattering of substance for several reasons, to be explained as this chapter unfolds, and was therefore taken up by the writer with a highly-qualified gas engineer, who had as one of his responsibilities the town gas supply to the Crystal Palace. Eminent in his field, and holding the position of Principal Distributing Engineer covering the South East Region, this gentleman asked that for professional reasons he should remain unnamed.

In several letters to the writer, this engineer has not only described details of the gas service to the Palace, but has also found himself at a loss to understand what Sir Henry Buckland was talking about when he spoke of a 'big gas container' adding that 'We most certainly never had any container or storage tank of any kind at the Crystal Palace. Even the gas meter was in a separate building.' Maybe this gas meter was the 'gas container' that Sir Henry was referring to.

Mr. H. M. Marsh, spent most of his working life as a maintenance plumber at the Palace. Having an intimate knowledge of the whole complex and its services, he was emphatic, when interviewed by the writer, that no gas container existed within the building, and at the same time confirmed that the gas meter was outside, and in a separate building.

Why then, did Sir Henry Buckland continue to be so emphatic that the reason for the fire was gas? Well, there is one possible answer. In May 1936, The Sydenham Gas Company advised Sir Henry Buckland that the Crystal Palace was losing gas by leakage to the equivalent of an annual cost of £400. In June 1936, the Board tested points of supply in the Reservoir meter, Egyptian Court meter and the 5-inch Exhibition main, and ascertained that 90 cubic feet of gas per hour was being lost through the 5-inch Exhibition main. They also shut off nearly 1,000 feet of old gas pipe. They said that there were a large number of gas pipes going to old and unused gaslight fittings. Sir Henry Buckland told the Board on 26th June that he had 'Given instructions to my staff to proceed with the work of removing disused pipelines, old gas lamps, brackets, etc.' He went on to say 'It is evident however, that we shall not even then have eradicated the trouble, and I intend to pursue the matter until I am satisfied that all leakages have been stopped'. As anticipated by Sir Henry, this exercise does not appear to have been very successful as he advised the Board in July that it 'had not been possible to reduce to any extent the amount of gas unaccounted for'. The Gas Company tested the pipes again in September 1936 and more than a dozen gas leaks were shut off in various areas such as the Ambassador's Room, the Concert Hall, Fine Art Store, Monkey House, Organ Grandstand, and the Persian Court. Discussions with the Gas Company were still ongoing at the end of October but without much success.

There was, however, nothing unorthodox about the Palace gas supply; it followed the normal practice for large buildings. Along Crystal Palace Parade, entrenched below ground, was an 8-inch nominal internal diameter main. This entered the Palace basement at the southern end to run the length of the building, it led gradually reduced to 5-inch nominal internal diameter as it neared the northern end of the structure, where it increased to 8-inch diameter as it turned outwards to rejoin the main in Crystal Palace Parade. My gas engineer states 'These valves, by the way, were closed by Gas Company staff when they were called to the fire'. Vertical connecting pipes probably made of wrought iron and of one-inch diameter were taken upwards from the main and through the floor of the Palace, bringing a ready and convenient supply to exhibitors. A control valve was fitted at the lower end of each connecting pipe, allowing for the gas supply to be cut off and the pipe to be removed when not required. Undoubtedly, some falling debris would have damaged these small pipes.

Originally, the Crystal Palace had been illuminated by gas, using 10,000 burners and 33,000 light globes. In the course of time gas illumination gave way to electricity, so that by 1936 only a few gaslights remained within the building, sufficient only to provide an emergency source of illumination.

The big gas 'container' existed only in Sir Henry Buckland's imagination, and nowhere else. Had such a container, or even one of Logie Baird's industrial gas bottles strayed for some reason near to where the fire started, there would most certainly have been an explosion of sufficient power to have injured, if not killed several people present, including Sir Henry Buckland himself.

No explosion occurred, and no one was injured; it was not until much later, when most of the building was down, that the explosions referred to in part four took place.

Outside however, on Crystal Palace Parade, there was a gas compressor house. Because one eyewitness testified to having observed long flames fed by something which, in the witness's opinion could have been flaming streams of gas coming from fractured piping (and he may well have been right, but for a different reason, as we shall see in due course), the writer's interest and suspicion fell for a time on the compressor house. What if someone had entered the house to tamper with the compressor, permitting its output pressure to be vastly increased? Could this cause some of the piping or joints to fail; thus allowing gas to escape in quantity and to ignite from whatever source was to hand? This possibility had the writer worried until the same gas engineer explained the nature and the purpose of the compressor. This was a small motor-driven fan rotating in-side a cylinder, producing a small increase in gas pressure between the inlet pipe and the outlet pipe of the compressor. The inlet pressure direct from the main was ½lbf/in2 and the outlet pressure from the compressor was 2lbf/in2; a mere 1½lb. Not enough to blow up a balloon, let alone burst wrought iron piping and jointing. This extra, insignificant increase in gas pressure was required to supply gas to certain gas lamps situated out on the terrace on the far side of the building and had no connection with the building's internal system. Thus, the writer would have been obliged to give up any further notions about gas, unless a straightforward accident had brought about a leakage of gas of a quantity large enough to be ignited by a spark, electrical or otherwise.

A close examination of the lath and plaster ceiling of any old building might well reveal badly-perished electrical cable with exposed conductors running alongside gas pipes. In the absence of any other means of ignition, we could be certain that arcing between the exposed electrical conductors would cause a fire. Could something like this have happened at Crystal Palace?

Undoubtedly the possibility exists, and must exist wherever gas and electricity come close together in the presence of oxygen, which is essential to all forms of combustion. However, in the case of the Crystal Palace the possibility is a remote one, given its mode of construction and that it was comparatively free from hidden cavities. There were no lath and plaster ceilings concealing gas piping and electrical circuits which, for the most part, were below floor level in the basement. The electrical wiring was carried in wooden boxes which had longitudinal slots in them, allowing for one wire only to each slot; by today's standards an old-fashioned method perhaps, but still a very efficient one. If, during an exhibition, a customer required a supply of electricity, then a connection was made to these wires and fed up through the floor. Wood being an excellent non-conductor, and with only one wire to each slot, the chance of an arc developing between two conductors would be virtually eliminated. There was no cavity or void beneath the main floor of the Crystal Palace, the timber planking forming both Palace floor and basement ceiling. The gas piping and the electrical circuits were therefore visible and exposed.

The most consistent complaint about the Palace centred around its incurable draughtiness, especially in winter. If this was so of the building itself, it was even more so of the basement, which was swept by the wind like a railway tunnel; in the event of fire, a serious impediment, but also a tremendous advantage in the event of a gas leak or seepage. The draughtiness of the Palace basement, and indeed the whole building, was enough to ensure it being continuously swept clear of any concentration or accumulation of gas sufficient, when combined with oxygen, to bring about an ignition unless that is, the leakage was sudden and massive, resulting not in fire, but almost certainly in a violent explosion – something which most positively did not occur. In the absence of cavities or voids where gas could concentrate and build up, and in the presence of a persistent breeze-swept environment, the case for a gas-triggered fire becomes extremely weak and without any viable foundation.

It can, therefore, only be concluded that Sir Henry Buckland was deceived, along with others, by what he saw, i.e. the streak of flame running along the room or, if they were not deceived as to the true nature of what they saw preferred, for some reason, to ignore it and remain silent. Otherwise it must be assumed that in the failure of others to come up with a precise answer as to what started the fire, Sir Henry Buckland, always having a keen eye on money, might have seen in his theory about gas the makings of a case for damages against the Sydenham Gas Company. The fact that no case was brought could be due to any number of reasons – his lack of any substantial evidence, the evidential fact that he knew gas was a problem in the building (certainly up to September 1936 and possibly after) and his sure knowledge that once in open court awkward questions about other aspects of the fire and building maintenance were certain to be raised.

No one could go so far as to rule out completely gas or electricity as possible culprits. Both are potential fire-raisers if incorrectly installed, wrongly used, or badly maintained; therefore both must be weighed and balanced along with, and in relation to, every other known aspect bearing on the case.

There was no explosion, and of that we can be certain. Whilst not dismissing gas or electricity out of hand, it is important for the reader to fully understand that gas – or electrically-triggered fires – which get out of control resulting in serious conflagration and widespread damage, almost always occur in premises which are unoccupied during the week or at weekends, in premises where the occupants are asleep or where, by reason of some manufacturing process, inflammable or explosive vapours may be present. Overloaded electrical circuits and related equipment, e.g. plugs, sockets, adapters or electric motors, normally give some advance warning of their condition, either by blown fuses or by undue heat accompanied by the unmistakable odour associated with burning or overheated insulation. Likewise, a gas leak of any consequence betrays its presence by the unique smell of town gas unless, of course, the premises in question are unoccupied, or with persons asleep. This was never the case with the Crystal Palace which even when completely closed to the public, was constantly patrolled by its own security force, night and day, seven days a week.

No manufacturing process giving rise to explosive or inflammable vapours was carried on there, so it is reasonable to expect that the security men would have recognised the telltale characteristics of gas or electrical systems approaching a dangerous and critical state. On the night of fire there were, besides security men, others present in the building when fire first showed itself. So by no stretch of the imagination could the Palace be deemed unoccupied. There were still several workmen just finishing a spell of overtime – erecting a boxing ring and arranging rows of chairs in the centre transept below and in front of the orchestra staging and the Great Organ; and in the basement, a few of Logie Baird's employees working overtime. In the Garden Lobby of the south transept, the Crystal Palace Orchestral Society's members, numbering thirty people, were arriving for a rehearsal in charge of their leader Mr. F.W. Holloway.

The late Mr. Sydney Clark, known as Horace by his colleagues and close friends, worked at the Crystal Palace for thirty-one years, except for a period of military service in France during the 1914-18 War. Mr. Clark is described by those who remember him as a modest, reliable and conscientious man who loved the Palace and was happy with his post there as a fire security man.

On the evening of 30th November 1936, Mr. Clark, along with a second security man, took over from the day shift, arriving a little before 7:00pm. The two men settled down to spend a long night-watch of twelve hours guarding the vast, darkened and somewhat ghostly glass house until they were relieved by three day-shift colleagues at 7:00am the next day.

The day shift handed the building over with everything apparently in order, and nothing unusual to report.

48

Practically on 7:00pm, Mr. Clark commenced his first patrol of the night. This took the form of a slow walk throughout the length of the south nave and transept, checking doors and windows, making sure that all were closed and secured, looking here and there for intruders and sniffing the air for a whiff of smoke or other signs of fire. Finding nothing untoward he arrived back at the firemen's office, which was located in the centre transept. He checked with his assistant, whose job was to maintain watch in the office and over the telephone, and then set out once more, this time in a northerly direction, to patrol the north nave with its historical and period Courts set back to left and right in the side aisles. The north nave would always take longer to check than would the more open south nave and transept. This was because each one of the period and historical Courts had to be searched individually both for intruders and for fire. Each Court was something of a maze, being full of partially concealed nooks and crannies behind the multitude of statuary, pillars and screens, which presented ideal cover for intruders and wrong-doers. Night security watch in the Crystal Palace was most certainly no job for those of a nervous or over-imaginative disposition.

With Mr. Clark setting out on his tour of the north nave we arrive at the point in this narrative where mystery, contradiction, and conflicting evidence begins.

According to an account of these events from the Crystal Palace Trustees, Mr. Clark first became aware of something amiss almost at the outset of his entry into the north nave. Immediately upon passing into the nave from its intersection with the centre transept, and hard on its left, was the Egyptian Court, where commenced the security check for this part of the building. When Mr. Clark reached the Egyptian Court he noticed a smell of smoke, but being unable to trace its source he went to the adjacent boiler house to attend the boiler. It should be noted that this boiler was completely separate and independent from the chain of boilers in the basement; it was intended only as a means of heating the administrative offices which ran along the back of the Egyptian Court, and looked out upon Crystal Palace Parade at a point just to the north of the centre transept. Having attended the boiler to his satisfaction, Mr. Clark returned to the Egyptian Court between 7:30 and 7:40pm, (the times are Mr. Clark's) and found the smoke increased. In the course of further search, which took him into a passage-way between the Court and the office section, he found the female staff mess-room well alight.

For an account of what happened next, I am grateful to Mr. Clark's widow. The words are Mrs. Clark's. 'My late husband was one of the two firemen on duty that night. He told me he was going his rounds, and had just passed the ladies' cloakroom when he noticed it was a blazing inferno. He asked the other man to turn on the hoses; they came on with such a force it knocked him down. They then telephoned Penge Fire Station, and there was some delay. I think the fire insurance had lapsed'.

Setting aside Mrs. Clark's last sentence for the time being, it is evident that Mr. Clark either used an internal telephone, or ran to the centre transept to call his colleague, Mr. Frank Tullett (or Nobby to his workmates). Just which of the above methods were used by Mr. Clark to call Frank Tullett we cannot be sure for lack of evidence. What we can be sure of, however, is that it was Mr. Clark who handled the hose, and held the nozzle and Mr. Tullett who operated the delivery valve admitting the water to the hose with such force as to throw Mr. Clark off balance and pitch him over, breaking his dentures and his spectacles in the process. We can be sure about that, for it is evidence confirmed by Mrs. Phyllis Griggs, Frank Tullett's daughter, and Mr. H. M. Marsh, maintenance plumber. Moreover it is testimony to Mr. Clark's honesty, for no man would like to admit being party to a fiasco, especially to his wife. They did eventually get the equipment to work without much difficulty, only having had a modicum of training. In the days of the Crystal Palace it was common for a hose to be of the type used by fire brigades, i.e. flat canvas which, in buildings, was not rolled but laid in overlapping loops and stowed on wooden pegs protruding from the wall. Water was admitted by means of a heavy, hand-operated valve, the hose itself being of 2 inches or 2½ inches diameter with a nozzle diameter of a quarter of an inch or half an inch. To get to work with that type of equipment, at least two men are required: one to run out the hose, the other to turn or open the valve. To carry out both actions the two operators would require to be trained to the same degree as professional fire brigade personnel and in the Crystal Palace that was the type of equipment provided.

We learnt earlier in this book that the fire hydrants were charged with water from tanks sited atop the two towers, at least 284ft above ground floor level and that the water was gravity-fed through 8-inch diameter mains. With such a system, the pressure at the hydrants would be enormous. It is the writer's opinion that with such a head pressure the jet thrust reaction at the nozzle would be so violent that a even a trained and experienced fireman might well find himself unable to hold on unaided.

Therefore, with two men on the nozzle a third man would be needed to open the valve, in which case Mr. Clark and Mr. Tullett were attempting the impossible. But if we assume that one man, correctly trained, could hold the nozzle, then his security would be dependent upon the second man opening the delivery valve slowly and smoothly, allowing him time in which to adjust his balance and stance in relation to the thrust reaction at the nozzle. We can, therefore, safely conclude that Mr. Clark was thrown over either because the task was beyond his strength, or because Mr. Tullett spun the delivery valve open with a rapid movement in undue but understandable haste to see water on the fire, or because lack of training left him knowing no better.

Once Mr. Clark failed to control the pipe, allowing it to break loose from his grip, he would have little chance of recovery. A free hose under pressure is a wicked contrivance. The heavy brass or gunmetal nozzle lashes rapidly and with terrible violence from side to side, perfectly capable of maiming and of killing. It will stop when the water is cut off, and that means closing the delivery valve – always assuming that one can get close enough before being struck down. To attempt it demands not only courage but also training and experience. For the untrained and inexperienced the exercise can be suicidal. Here, it was probably impossible of achievement by Mr. Clark and his assistant, shocked by the sudden appearance of fire itself and with their confidence undermined by their failure to bring the hose into positive action. The situation would have been made worse by their being alone and faced with forces which they did not understand and were not trained to deal with.

There will be those who consider that Mr. Clark's first mistake was not his failure to call the fire brigade when he first saw fire in the ladies' cloakroom, but his failure to persist with his search for the source of the smoke which he could smell when he entered the Egyptian Court. He abandoned his search in order to attend to the boiler which heated the office section.

In this age of automatic oil-fired central heating plant, which runs itself for long periods without attention, and a 'failsafe' if trouble should develop, it is easy to forget that in 1936, heating boilers were hand-fired with solid fuel, either coke or anthracite. At night it was normal practice to bank up the furnace with fuel, setting the dampers on low draught so as to ensure the fire remained alight, but burning slowly throughout the night. In the morning, it required only that the dampers be opened for the furnace to brighten up, and the temperature to rise.

It was one of Mr. Clark's duties to tend that boiler, and there can be no dispute here, for there was no one else to do it between 7:00pm and 7:00am the next day. It would be convenient for Mr. Clark to look in at the boiler whilst on his way round the building. It would also be provident for him to do so, in order to check that the boiler remained in a safe condition. In fact, it would be highly improvident for any security man not to visit a boiler house within his area of responsibility; such neglect would be a gross and hazardous irresponsibility.

Mr. Clark was perfectly correct in his action of visiting the boiler-house, not only to tend it, but to assure himself that some malfunction of the boiler was not responsible for the smell of smoke in the Egyptian Court. Mr. Clark made no mention of being able to see smoke, only that he could smell it. At that stage, and with no visible explanation for the smell, two conclusions present themselves: (a) that the smell of smoke was carried on the air from some source outside the building or (b) that it emanated from a source within the building other than the immediate surroundings of the Egyptian Court. The boiler-house being close by it would be at once suspect, for it was the abode of the only controlled and legitimate fire in the building – the boiler furnace. The set of boilers in the basement were not lit that night. For reasons of strict economy they were lit only prior to some public function taking place, the next of which was not due until later in the week, as stated by the Palace boiler-man to the Daily Telegraph newspaper on Wednesday 2nd December 1936.

Had Mr. Clark been properly trained in firemanship, he may well have been able to see smoke and the direction of its drift, instead of only smelling it. To do that he would have had to switch off all illumination in the Egyptian Court, and then probe the air with the beam from an electric torch. In a condition of total darkness, with the absence of shadow, faint drifting smoke invisible in strong illumination can become both visible and directional in the beam of a good torch.

Failure to call the fire brigade immediately upon the discovery of an outbreak has resulted in the ruin of more property than any other single contributory factor; and so it was with the Crystal Palace. Many decades of practical experience have taught professional firemen that, as a general rule of thumb, the first ten minutes of a building fire and the correctness or otherwise of the action taken can decide whether the building is to be saved or lost. This measurement of time is not rigid and therefore must not be taken as common to every circumstance. Different types of buildings and their contents will determine their flammability or resistance to fire.

The ten-minute parameter is therefore a generalisation, allowing for reasonable time-lapse from the moment at which an early stage fire is discovered, quickly assessed, the fire brigade called, first-aid measures taken whilst awaiting their arrival and the moment when the positive offensive attack of the fire brigade begins to have remediable effect on the whole situation. After the lapse of ten minutes, and in the absence of the remediable effect, a rapidly worsening and deteriorating sequence sets in, creating a situation which becomes progressively more difficult to deal with as each minute passes. Paxton was sufficiently aware of the possibility of fire in his building to include a high-pressure drencher system above the roof so that water could flood over the glass fabric in the event of fire. The fact that the equipment had fallen into disuse long before 1936 was not his fault.

What then was the reason for Mr. Clark's failure to call the fire brigade at once? Whatever the reason, it resulted in a delay of anything between 19 and 29 minutes depending on which of the times were assumed to be correct – 7:30 or 7:40. We shall, however, discover in due course that this delay was, in fact, much longer.

The private fire security patrol at the Crystal Palace was uniformed and, to a certain extent, organised and disciplined but, as we have seen, its weakness lay uppermost in its lack of practical instruction in the use of the equipment provided. It is fair to assume therefore that its members would to some extent be security minded, and probably aware of the need not to delay calling the fire brigade.

To be aware is not the same thing as being able to act on or make use of awareness. It is in this difference that one may find a possible and, probably the most likely, explanation for Mr. Clark's delay.

The security personnel were denied the freedom of action even when such action was based on common sense. This existed in the form of Sir Henry Buckland, the General Manager of the Crystal Palace who, in turn, was the victim of an economic tyranny which expected him to run an institution on behalf of a nation not prepared to allocate him a penny of public money. While allowing him that, it must be remembered that Sir Henry got the job at the Palace primarily on his proven ability to get the Royal Spa Establishment at Harrogate 'off the rates' and to run it at a profit. Sir Henry had, therefore, solved the financial problems at one loss-making establishment, only to walk straight into another.

In order to carry through the restoration, and keep the place going on income accrued at the turnstiles and booking office, he had to slash costs wherever possible, and to guard against costs being incurred without his direct sanction. In 1936, one sure way of incurring costs at the Crystal Palace was to get involved with the London Fire Brigade.

We have learnt of the establishment, on 1st January 1866, of the Metropolitan Fire Brigade, and the transfer of men and equipment from the insurance companies. In order to satisfy legal requirements, the transfer needed an Act of Parliament, which was passed in 1865 and described as the Metropolitan Fire Brigade Act, 1865. Section 30 of the Act reads as follows: 'It shall he lawful for the Board, when Occasion requires, to permit any Part of the Fire Brigade Establishment, with their Engines, Escapes, and other Implements, to proceed beyond the Limits of the Metropolis for the Purpose of extinguishing Fires. In such Case the Owner and Occupier of the Property where the Fire has occurred shall be jointly and severally liable to defray all the Expenses that may be incurred by the Fire Brigade in attending the Fire, and shall pay to the Board a reasonable Charge for the Attendance of the Fire Brigade, and the Use of their Engines, Escapes, and other Implements.'

The merits or otherwise of the Act are no longer of relevance, the Act itself being long-since defunct. It is very obvious that the concluding sentence of Section 30 must, in its day, have posed a serious dilemma for the occupier of a place of public entertainment – someone who is almost always the licensee, and in turn is almost always the general manager. The occupier, as distinct from the owner could, in the event of a dispute or in the case an unscrupulous owner, find himself responsible for defrayment of the whole of the fire brigade expenses.

The Crystal Palace was the property of the nation, on whose behalf it was administered by a board of trustees. As representatives of the nation, they might be described as being the middlemen between owner and occupier. The occupier was very definitely Henry James Buckland, although he came to think of himself as the owner, always referring to the place as, 'my Crystal Palace.' Nor was his ownership complex confined to mere verbal expression.

By nature, Sir Henry Buckland was the complete autocrat, the monarch of the Crystal Palace who paid scant reference to the trustees and engaged in almost continuous battle with them over matters of policy; battles which, in the end, he almost always won. To him, the Board of Trustees was little more than a well-meaning irrelevancy that was wholly unable to manage the day-to-day affairs of the Crystal Palace. There were few, if any among them, able to stand up to his arrogance, his biting tongue, and his undisguised scorn.

As time went on, and particularly after his knighthood, his position became unassailable by virtue of his achievement of saving the Palace, so that in the end he was left almost entirely to his own devices. His foremost preoccupation was with garnering and nurturing monetary resources for the continued improvement and embellishment of his beloved glass palace.

It is often said that one can kill by kindness or by an excess of love. If ever that were true, it was certainly the case with Sir Henry and his relationship with his Crystal Palace; in the end, his obsession with its financial well-being… well-being became self-defeating and self-destructive. Knowing of the Metropolitan Fire Brigade Act, and of the significance for the Palace, situated as it was beyond the limits of the Metropolis, he had made a standing order. This forbade any member of the staff, including all fire security personnel, from calling the fire brigade, no matter what the circumstances, without his personal sanction or, in his absence, the sanction of his confidential private secretary Mr. Sydney Legg. Of course neither of them was qualified to make such a decision, but it is excusable when it is realised that on the 29th May 1937 Sir Henry received a bill from the London Fire Brigade for £2,569. 13s 7d. This being their charge for their attendance at the fire.

To appreciate the devastating and paralysing effect of that standing order on Mr. Clark, and his colleagues, we must understand the relationship between employer and employee. Even in terms of the present, Sydenham and district lacks local industry sufficient for the employment of its residents, most of whom travel further afield to find work. In the years before its destruction, the Crystal Palace was the hub from which all else radiated for miles around, providing both status and prosperity over a wide area; with its destruction came the end of that status and prosperity. With the Palace gone, the heart was also gone, leaving a vacuum which has yet to be filled, having stubbornly remained so for years. To appreciate the blight which followed the downfall of the Palace one only has to look around and consider the roads lined with what were once fine and dignified houses now, for the most part, converted to flats. Its exalted position over so long a period and its gradual restoration had, by 1936, brought the Crystal Palace to a point where it had become the biggest single employer of labour in the district. To have a job in the Crystal Palace, whether it be full or part-time, was to have security in a viable and highly celebrated concern at a time when there was precious-little security, or work, for that matter, elsewhere.

To have a job at the Palace was one thing, but to keep it was another – dependent entirely on whether or not your face fitted with Sir Henry Buckland. If your face failed to fit or you courted his displeasure, you were quickly out in the cold with no job, in what was then a jobless world; a world in which today's social security setup was only the dream of left wing politicians and liberal reformers. Moreover, there was no such thing as a contract of employment or wrongful dismissal, and the trades unions were without recognition in Sir Henry's scheme of things.

During the course of research for this book, the writer was able, after some difficulty, to talk with Sir Henry Buckland's surviving family – his widow Lady Buckland, and his daughters Irene and Chrystal all of whom, besides showing much kindness, were forthcoming and helpful. All three are agreed that Sir Henry was a hard taskmaster, demanding and getting both hard work and loyalty from his employees or, in default of either, sacking them on the spot: 'My father had no time for slackers' was how Irene expressed it, 'father would sack them on the spot and without notice.'

The word slacker, however, had a wide interpretation for Sir Henry and could include anyone who was reckless enough to countermand or to disobey his standing orders. On the other hand, and in fairness to Sir Henry, if he liked an employee and if he considered them to be hard working and loyal, then he could be extremely kind and would, on occasion, worry himself and go to unusual lengths on their behalf. If sickness or other difficulty laid them off work, he would fret for their welfare and give them money from his own pocket to tide them over a bad spot. Thus, by means of an autocratic tyranny tinged with benevolence, he was able to tie people to him and to depend upon them for loyalty to a remarkable degree, particularly when viewed from a modern standpoint.

Having seen how Sir Henry operated his brand of labour relations, we can surely understand and sympathise with Mr. Clark's decision to stick to the standing orders and inform his superiors, rather than to call the fire brigade on his own initiative. The way in which he informed his superiors is less easy to understand, unless one has lived in an age before the telephone.

It would appear that he dispatched his colleague, Frank Tullett, on foot, to alert Sir Henry's Secretary, Sydney Legg, who in lived in a flat in the old Crystal Palace Fire Station just north of the main entrance on Crystal Palace Parade and then alerted Sir Henry, who lived in the mansion 'Rockhills'. This used to be the residence of Sir Joseph Paxton and was located on the corner of West Hill (now Westwood Hill) and Crystal Palace Parade, a considerable distance from where the fire was discovered.

When reporting the sequence of events, newspaper accounts are at variance over time, but they roughly agree on substance, except for a few notable inconsistencies which we will consider in due course.

Sir Henry Buckland had just finished dinner when, at sometime between 7:15 and 8:00pm, (for such is the degree of variance evident in the newspaper times) he went out either to post a letter, or to exercise his dogs, or both. He took with him his daughter Chrystal. On turning out of 'Rockhills' he saw a red glow behind the office section of the Palace. He thought at once of fire, and hurried to the main entrance of the building, along with his daughter.

Chrystal Buckland was only a young girl in 1936. Being so young, and the effect that this might have on memory can result in distortion – a factor which I have had to constantly bear in mind and which has frequently proved a worry when questioning witnesses. One can but allow for it, use one's instinct and try to tread the middle ground, always wary of any pitfall. However, Chrystal was both an intelligent and easy person with whom to talk, and patently honest in so far as memory and knowledge allow her to be. She said that she cannot be sure of the time, but thinks that 7:30pm is about right for when she left the house with her father. She is very sure about what she saw and what she was doing in the next few minutes, the shock of events having burned a deep brand on the mind of a young girl: 'When we reached the building we found a small fire in the ladies' cloakroom at the rear of the Egyptian Court, which was being tackled by some men. My father instructed me to go and tell the orchestra that there was a fire, but to continue with their rehearsal as it was only small and under control, and that there was no danger.' To carry out her father's instruction she had to walk at a quick pace across the centre transept, and down the full length of the south nave, passing Osler's Crystal Fountain and the Great Clock before making a sharp left turn in to the Garden Hall of the south transept: 'To cover the distance, deliver father's message and set out on my return to the south nave required no more than three or four minutes; no more than four minutes, certainly. That is why I was so amazed when, upon re-entering the south nave, I saw the intersection with the centre transept to be a mass of flames. In such a short time... I have always been puzzled by that and have never been able to understand it. I ran back at once and told the orchestra to get out quickly'.

Chrystal's estimate of between three and four minutes for her journey proved to be amazingly accurate. When re-enacted by the author, it took a fraction over three minutes. It could, however, have been four minutes, depending on how long Chrystal spent in conversation with members of the orchestra.

Something else which Chrystal could not understand at the time was meeting Frank Tullett running up Crystal Palace Parade towards 'Rockhills'; 'While father and I were hurrying towards the main entrance we met Mr. Tullett coming towards us up the Parade. Why was he running up the road towards father and me? I should have thought that his place was inside the building helping to fight the fire'.

I was unable to answer her question at this time, and was conscious that in some way she expected me to be able to provide an answer to something which had puzzled her all her life. At that time, I was not aware of Sir Henry's standing orders and I had still to contact Mr. Clark's widow and Frank Tullett's daughter. Like Chrystal, I had yet to learn of the accident with the hose. Quite obviously, she had never had an explanation from her father. All this leaves an unanswered question: why waste time running around outside the building looking for someone in authority when telephones must have been to hand?

Several possible explanations present themselves: In order to guard against illicit use of the telephone by Palace employees, access to an outside line was not allowed after normal business hours, some malfunction of the telephone system itself, making contact with 'Rockhills' impossible, or simply shock reaction, paralysing the mental process to the extent that neither Mr. Clark nor Mr. Tullett could, in their confusion, remember the 'Rockhills' number, or where to find it written down.

The first explanation is unlikely for the reason that a private wire to 'Rockhills' could easily have been provided for, without giving access to the outside. Malfunction of the telephone circuitry is unlikely, unless of course the fire had already burned through some part of the wiring, thus effectively cutting off the entire system. The third explanation requires some consideration. The paralysing effect to the mental process in sudden, unexpected fire situations is a common phenomenon resulting in a manner of irrational behaviour, especially where regular drills and practised instruction have been lacking or allowed to lapse.

We have already seen how Mr. Clark had experienced a nasty double impact. The shock of finding the fire and the shock, both mental and physical, of being thrown over by the hose, some of which must have rubbed off on Frank Tullett.

If we dismiss the above explanation, it would seem that we are left with two alternatives. Either Frank Tullett 'phoned 'Rockhills' some few seconds after Sir Henry Buckland and his daughter had left the house, and thought that if he ran outside he might just catch them coming along the Parade, or a sophisticated arson conspiracy had seen to it that the telephones were made inoperative before the fire was set.

In the event of a straightforward accident, the former would seem reasonable enough. On the other hand, if the latter were the case, then of course all the foregoing alternatives would become irrelevant and if it could be proved beyond all doubt that the telephones had been cut...; of that we may never be certain. Only Mr. Clark or Mr. Tullett could perhaps enlighten us, and both are dead. Even if it were possible to talk to either, it is difficult to see how they could know whether the telephones were out because of fire damage, or cut before the fire commenced if, in fact, either were the case. We would have to have some part of the telephone wiring and a skilled fire investigator to be sure.

Let us for a while consider a random selection of newspaper reports for Tuesday 1st December 1936 the day following the fire. If we examine the various statements directly attributed to Sir Henry Buckland, we at once become aware of a remarkable degree of contradiction, both on time and on subject matter. On the former,

Sir Henry ranges between times as wide apart as 7:15 – 8:00pm, the time when he first saw the fire, although 7:25 – 7:30pm appears more often.

The *Daily Herald* quotes Sir Henry as follows: 'I saw a red glow and raced along to the seat of the fire, shouting for the three firemen who were on duty. The firemen and my daughter responded at once. While the firemen attacked the flames, my daughter ran across to the other side of the Palace where the Palace orchestra was rehearsing. They got the south doors open and escaped that way.' Reasonable enough so far as it goes, and in a general way agreeing with the account given to the author by Chrystal Buckland.

The Daily Telegraph quotes him differently: 'I had just left my house at the end of the north aisle of the Palace to go out to dinner when I saw flames in the Egyptian section at the back of my office. I ran into the building and saw that my two firemen of the Palace staff were already trying to extinguish the flames. It was incredible the way the flames took hold of the building. I saw them sweeping up the glass walls and could see at once that the Palace was doomed. I hastened down to the central concert hall, where the Crystal Palace Orchestral

Society were practicing for a concert, and ordered them to leave the building by the south aisle exit.'

Here already we can see emerging, like a fog, a pattern of conflicting evidence from the same person. The Herald has him '...shouting for the three firemen who were on duty.' The Daily Telegraph has him seeing that 'my two firemen were already trying to extinguish the flames.' We know that one of his firemen had already been thrown over by the hose and that, according to his daughter, the second fireman had met him outside on Crystal Palace Parade. In the Herald his daughter is helping the orchestra to escape from the other side of the Palace. In the Telegraph, Sir Henry himself is 'ordering the orchestra to leave the central concert hall.'

As far as the orchestra is concerned, Chrystal's account is positively confirmed, as we shall see shortly, by members of the orchestra. Unfortunately, for the memory of her late father, there is no confirmation to be found anywhere for his story. The Daily Mirror quotes Sir Henry as being generally in agreement with his daughter's account. He finds 'two of his three night-duty firemen already at work with a high-pressure hose.' The main points of difference here being that he had 'just finished his dinner,' whereas in the Daily Telegraph he is 'going out to dinner,' and that one of his firemen has vanished altogether as if he had never existed, which in fact he hadn't. As we have seen, there were only two, Mr. Clark, and Mr. Tullett.

When we come to look at the Star, we find Sir Henry telling a story which, in substance, bears very little relationship to any of the others. He was out walking with his daughter Chrystal when he saw flames at 7:50pm 'We got to the entrance, and the fire was already raging across the roof... my firemen were there and they were doing all they could. I still hoped we could beat it. Fire engines were arriving all the time, but it wasn't long before I could see the building was lost.' No small fire in a ladies' cloakroom, no red flames in the Egyptian section at the back of his office but fire raging uncontrolled across the roof. No mention either of a rehearsing orchestra, or where they were supposed to be – in the central concert hall, or the Garden Hall of the south transept. They were most certainly not in the central concert hall, which was part of the great centre transept, with flames raging over their heads.

The remarkable thing about this story is its accuracy when related to time. At 7:50pm flames were undoubtedly raging across the roof. If we recall earlier in this book, we will remember that the first call for help was received by Penge Fire Brigade at 7:59pm, and that at 8:00pm, Major Morris could see from the balcony of his flat at London Fire Brigade Headquarters that the centre transept was well alight. Penge Fire Brigade arrived at just before 8.03pm to find the centre transept ablaze from end to end and from ground to roof.

Someone once said that 'time is a thief'. Nowhere is this more so than during the high drama of sudden emergency, and it would seem to Sir Henry, if in fact he was there, that at 7:50pm fire engines were arriving all the time; especially if he found the roof well alight. Arriving at so critical a time he might not, in the heat of the moment, notice any passage of time. That would most certainly hold valid if he engaged himself in a frantic search of the building to ascertain that no one was trapped. That he would do so, would not be out of character. For all his defects, factual and supposed, no one can say that he lacked courage or that he was afraid for himself.

He had spent a goodly part of his life courageously fighting for what he believed to be right, and for those for whom he felt responsible; he would not desert either his employees or his patrons if he thought their lives to be in jeopardy. Whilst so absorbed, he would not be conscious of time having taken wings, making 7.50pm become 8.00pm and just afterwards, when fire engines did start arriving.

Which, if any, of Sir Henry's stories are we to believe? And why the differing stories both of substance and of time? His daughter is not sure about the time, but she is sure about what she saw and did; and because of this and a partial verification by members of the orchestra, we may be tempted into believing that her father's arrival fits 7:25-7:30pm rather than the later one of 7:50pm.

If we glance at the Daily Express we see the other extreme in time, although not in fact, as we shall discover in due course. To an Express staff reporter Sir Henry Buckland spoke thus: 'I left the office at half-past five, and everything was alright then. The only occupants of the Palace were our own fire brigade and a musical society who were practicing'.

'At 7:15pm I went out to post a letter after dinner and saw a flame behind the offices, which are in the centre of the main building, almost on Crystal Palace Parade. I hurried in and found my firemen already at work.'

'I then hurried to warn the musicians, and they and their instruments were safely got out.'

No mention of his daughter or the number of firemen. Just a brief statement, important in as much as he is on the scene thirty-five minutes earlier than the Star has him at 7:50pm.

We cannot ignore the existence of journalistic licence in all these reports. Nor can we ignore the conditions, or the state of mind in which Sir Henry Buckland found himself when being questioned by so many frantic newsmen. For the many readers who have never seen a big fire, it is important that they should try to appreciate that clear verbal communication is difficult on or near the fire-ground, because of noise. There is the noise of the fire itself, and the noise of crashing debris, added to which is the noise of the fire pumps assuming a continuous roar, which increases in tumult as each successive pump arrives and is set into its water source. So we would have a situation where Sir Henry Buckland would probably have to shout to make himself clear to his listeners. Combine that with a distraught mind watching a lifetime's work being destroyed in a couple of hours, and it becomes easy to allow Sir Henry considerable room for inaccuracy, and unclear speech containing unintentional and seeming contradiction. A man can have very little time, if any, for reporters, if that same man is watching his house burn down. It is very often the case that professional showmen are extremely emotional under great stress and, if nothing else, Sir Henry Buckland was the showman par-excellence.

I would doubtless have been pondering still, and procrastinating over these conflicting statements of Sir Henry's, had the Daily Mirror not come to my rescue by very kindly publishing a letter which I had written appealing for assistance from anyone able to throw light on the Crystal Palace affair. My problem was how to break out of the seemingly intractable circle posed by Sir Henry's conflicting statements as to when the fire started. Within hours of my letter's publication my telephone commenced ringing and my letterbox began filling with mail, some of which was to destroy forever any faith which I may have had in press accounts of what Sir Henry was saying and doing, between 6:53pm and 8:00pm on that tragic night.

I was soon to discover the amazing possibility, indeed the near certainty, that this fire was under way as early as 6:45pm and that there was only one Palace fireman on duty rather than two or three as Sir Henry Buckland would have it, and as I previously believed it to be. The fireman was Mr. Clark, and only Mr. Clark. The second man, Mr. Tullett was not a fireman as Chrystal Buckland had thought, but a Crystal Palace attendant and general handyman who, finding Mr. Clark on duty alone, had apparently offered to stop back late and watch the office at least until Mr. Clark had completed his first patrol of the building, or until such time as another man showed up.

This strange circumstance became all too evident upon receipt of a letter from Mr. Tullett's daughter, and verbal verification by Mr. H. M. Marsh the plumber, who knew Frank Tullett as an attendant and general hand. When Frank Tullett made his offer of help to Mr. Clark, we can only assume that he could have had no idea of the desperate role cast for him that night by a cruel fate which was to place him on the delivery valve to the hose line; a position for which he had no training and for which he had not asked.

One may now well question by what throw of fate Mr. Clark had been earmarked to be alone on that night, of all nights. Or was fate being manipulated by some unseen hand? No one can deny that it would be expecting a lot of coincidence for Mr. Clark's regular colleague to have gone sick, or otherwise absented himself without warning his employer in good time for a replacement to have been found. Such disloyalty could have only resulted in instant dismissal according to Sir Henry's code of practice.

When Sir Henry spoke of finding two of his firemen already at work we must assume that, in the heat of the moment, he mistook Frank Tullett for someone else.

When he spoke of his three firemen, it would suggest that he was in the building before 7:00pm when the three day-shift firemen went off duty, or that between 7:15 and 7:30pm he had become so confused as to lose all track of time, causing him to believe the time to be earlier than it was, and the day-shift still at their posts.

At this point, an explanation is due as to why, earlier in this chapter, I gave the clear impression that Frank Tullett was a Palace fireman. The reason for this is that at the time of writing that part of the chapter I believed Frank Tullett to be just that. It was only later, when I had made contact with his daughter and Mr. Marsh, that I became aware of my error. I have, in this case, purposely allowed the error to remain as an example of the frustrating and devious paths which I have been forced to tread in my search for the truth.

The evidence of members of the orchestra rehearsing in the Garden Hall of the south transept is consistent, and dramatically illustrates how very close they came to disaster.

Had their escape been delayed by a few minutes, serious injury and worse could not have escaped them. Mr. Frank Holloway, who was organist at the Palace, told the press that, 'Thirty members of the orchestra were rehearsing, when shortly before eight o'clock Miss Chrystal Buckland told me that there was a fire, but that there was no danger. We carried on playing 'A Tale of Old Japan', but five minutes later we were warned that things were becoming hot and we had better clear out immediately. The whole of the Handel Festival's, music library had to be abandoned as well as music by other composers. There were many original manuscripts, worth many thousands of pounds. It is possible that some of Handel's original manuscripts were among those which had to be left, but I am not certain of this.'

If, in fact, there were original manuscripts in the Palace, then they should have been kept in a fireproof and waterproof strong room. Those responsible for a failure to see to that simple precaution would be guilty of neglect.

Mr. Holloway's account corroborates what Chrystal Buckland told the author in everything but time. Bearing in mind that she cannot be sure of the time, but thinks that 7:30pm is about right, it would seem that there was a considerable delay between her entering the building with her father and her going to warn the orchestra; unless they entered the building at the later time of 7:50pm as quoted by the Star. By this time, flames were raging across the roof, the time of the small fire had long passed, and the orchestra should have been clear of the building. It is inconceivable, having once met Chrystal, that she could ever be callous to the extent of disregarding the life of anyone, or anything, and I would believe it to be far removed from the nature of her father. For that reason we must dismiss from our minds the Star report. This is not to say that the Star or any of its staff acted dishonestly or irresponsibly. The Star was an evening newspaper printed on the day after the fire, and late in the afternoon, by which time Sir Henry would be calmer and able to reflect on what he had said earlier and on the previous night. He must, by this time, have decided that the circumstances of the fire left many unanswered questions and that the less he appeared to know about it the better for all concerned, in pursuance of which, he must have told the Star reporters of his late arrival; too late to have seen the fire in its formative stage and to judge its cause. A diplomatic subterfuge rather than a premeditated lie, and one which, in the circumstances, he was probably well advised to make. Had he made it from the outset, it would have stood a chance of being effective. As it was, it served only to discredit Sir Henry's earlier statements and to foment adverse and dangerous rumour, which had it that he had set the fire himself in order to benefit from the insurance; an idea as ridiculous as it was cruel, and something which I will demolish as a non-starter when we come to look closer at the whole question of insurance. For the time being, we shall return to the orchestra.

Mr. W. H. Honner of Beckenham told the Daily Telegraph that they got out just before the centre transept fell. They had been rehearsing since 7:30pm. At about 8:15pm a girl employee told them that a fire had broken out, but that there was no danger.

Five minutes later one of the female members of the orchestra went out to see if her car was safe. She returned to tell them that the Palace was well ablaze above the centre transept.

'We all ran to the entrance on the left of the centre transept', said Mr. Honner. 'As I was getting out on to the Parade, the front of the centre transept fell right out on to the road, in one great mass. We all had narrow escapes and had a hard job to get clear.

'My car was left by the main entrance, and I ran along there to see if I could get it. As I did so, the transept fell, and my car was gone.

'Mr. F. H. White, the secretary, also lost his car, which had been standing near mine.'

Mr. Honner's 'girl employee' was obviously Chrystal Buckland, as no female staff were on duty that night, being required only when the Palace was open to the general public. His story is further testimony to the truth of Miss Buckland's statement to the author and portrays the shock she felt when, returning to the south nave, she saw up ahead of her a mass of flames engulfing the intersection with the centre transept.

In a building of such massive proportions, it is difficult to understand such rapid and such violent flame – spread in the short space of four to five minutes, and all emanating from a small fire in a ladies' cloakroom some distance from the inflammable timber fixtures of the centre transept.

The orchestra's double bass was Mr. George Morris, of Kenley, Surrey. Mr. Morris has very kindly described, in a letter to this writer, his own particular experience and writes as follows: 'We, the orchestra were rehearsing in the Garden Hall of the Crystal Palace that night of the fire and the young lady first violin was called out for ten minutes, and when she came back our conductor Mr. Holloway called 'all out please.' I said to the French horn player next to me, I suppose we are going to play elsewhere. He replied, 'I expect so.' Then, looking out of the window I saw flames reflected on the glass of the north tower. Oh, look here, it's a fire. And so it was. All the players had fled, the flute, then violins and cellos, leaving me with my double bass case to put on. When this was done, I brought it out with me, and the glass was falling, and also the water from the firemen's hoses was coming in.'

'When I got to the door, I looked back to see if anyone was left inside. I could see only a thick mist, so I slammed the door shut behind me. The Palace was opened by Queen Victoria in 1854, and closed by George Morris on 30th November 1936! When I got outside, the Duke of Kent was watching, but soon went. My car, left in the main entrance, was gone. I telephoned the AA several times, but they could not find it. After two weeks Gipsy Hill police rang me to ask me if I could collect my car from them.'

George Morris's account confirms roughly the arrival time of the fire brigade as being close to 8:00pm, for although he does not mention time in his letter, he does describe how water from fire hoses was coming into the building. Taking that with Mr. Holloway's account of being ordered out of the building shortly before 8:05pm, it substantiates Penge Fire Brigade's arrival time of about 8:03pm. By the time Mr. Holloway and his fellow musicians had gathered up their instruments and reached the entrance, both the Penge pump and Beckenham's two pumps would have had water on the fire.

While certainly establishing the matter of time beyond reasonable doubt, George Morris's account and those of his colleagues raises an important question. Why, immediately upon arrival were the Penge firemen not ordered to carry out a search of the building to ensure that no persons were trapped?

The order of priority for all fire brigades has always been the saving of life first and property second. Early in my research, three fire officers were able between them to help trace for me one of the firemen who rode on that first pump from Penge Fire Station. Station Officer Bream of Beckenham had on his staff a Mr. Stone, who turned out to be the son of Mr. Albert Stone, who was one of those riding that first Penge pump.

Mr. Stone, turned out of Penge Fire Station on that memorable night with seven colleagues, commanded by Chief Officer J. Goodman. They arrived at Crystal Palace Parade at 8:03pm. They were confronted by an alarming and totally unexpected situation.

For Mr. Stone it was momentarily a question of whether or not to believe the evidence of his own eyes, for here was the whole huge central section, the main hall of the Crystal Palace, a raging mass of fire. The flames were through the roof and roaring outwards through the great arched west front. Apart from bystanders, already building into a crowd, there was no official of the Palace, no Palace firemen and no Sir Henry Buckland to be seen anywhere; not a sign, in fact, of anyone who could tell the Penge firemen what had happened, or whether or not persons were, or had been in the building. One thing was very obvious. If anyone was in the centre transept, they would have long since passed beyond mortal help and, as Mr. Stone, put it: 'There was only one thing for it – to get water on to the fire as quickly as we knew how, for to have entered the building at that point would have been asking for a quick funeral, and therefore, in view of that, and in the absence of anyone reporting persons trapped, no search was called for.'

By now, the Beckenham pumps had stopped outside the south transept and were connecting into hydrants close by. At the same time the musicians were emerging from the south doors, and no doubt would be telling the Beckenham firemen that all had got clear. There was, therefore no reason, by any accepted standard, to institute a search as such although, in practice, Beckenham firemen were already pushing forward into the south transept and up the south nave running out hose as they went, in the hope of stopping fire advancing in to the nave.

While all this was in progress, Croydon's turntable ladder was arriving to 'shoot a fireman' one hundred feet into the air in front of the centre transept so as to direct a jet of water into the main fire, and Mr. Stone had reached the top of an escape ladder pitched about 30ft up on the glass wall of the north nave, at a point just to the north of the centre transept. Mr. Stone's plan was to jet water into the nave in an effort to prevent the fire moving northward. His position was one of some difficulty. A heavy hose had to be manhandled, along with its gunmetal branch pipe and nozzle, up the ladder and secured. From above him, water was pouring down and soaking his uniform. This water was probably coming from the turntable ladder jet falling short of its objective, the result of an already troublesome water situation.

To get a jet into the building, Mr. Stone had to smash an access hole and decided to do this by cutting away the ornamental wooden pelmet which ran along the top of each horizontal run of glass. When he went to work with his axe, the timber was so badly rotted that it gave no resistance, and this allowed it to shoot forward, bringing Mr. Stone's right hand and forefinger into violent contact with the mess of rotten wood. To this day he carries the scar on his forefinger where a large splinter made entry.

Having made his access hole and enlarged it to allow room to manoeuvre, Mr. Stone could see inside an inferno of roaring fire moving along with the ferocity of a blowtorch: 'Something was behind and feeding those flames, I am certain of that. They were not the ordinary type of flame like you associate with burning woodwork, paper and the like. I think that it may well have been gas which was feeding those flames'.

Such is Mr. Stone's comment on what he was able to see inside the building. He also saw something on the outside of the building which struck as strange: 'Looking down on the outside, I was able to see into a small walled-off area which was without a roof. Inside, was a gas meter with a valve, or cock on the piping. There were two men struggling with the valve trying, I suppose, to turn off the gas. I looked down again after a minute or so, curious to see how they were getting on. Both men had gone, disappeared completely. I never saw them again and I have no idea who they were or where they came from, or whether or not they were Palace workers.'

'It seemed to me a bit late in the day for them to be trying to shut off gas. I should have thought that one of the first things to be done on discovery of the fire would have been to isolate all gas supplies. That is why seeing those two men has always struck me as being strange, especially in view of the advanced state of the fire and the time that it must have been going.'

They might have been South Eastern Gas Board engineers from Croydon who had been at an office dance at a local hotel. As soon as they heard about the fire they immediately went to the Palace still wearing their dinner jackets and carrying valve position drawings for the building. It is also known that they were helping out, turning off valves and performing other emergency actions. Whoever they were, we know that they did not shut off the gas. As the last chapter relates, Sydenham Gas Company workmen had to dig up the road to accomplish that.

Why did they not succeed in shutting off the gas? Was the valve jammed? Had conducted heat from inside the blazing transept already heated the piping and the valve, making it too hot to handle'? Were they in fact there to shut off the gas and if not, what then? Only they can tell us.

One might also ask why was it that they vanished so quickly and so silently from the scene without shouting in recognition, or perhaps some form of explanation to Mr. Stone? It would have been the natural thing to do in the circumstances, if only to warn Mr. Stone of their presence below him where broken glass or timber could easily injure them once Mr. Stone set to with his axe. From the roadway, they would be securely hidden from view by the retaining wall of the meter house. Did the impending danger from the fire dictate their sudden and rapid retreat, or did the sudden appearance of a fireman above them on a ladder, from where they could be seen, threaten to break their cover and expose their reason for being there? What if the gas had been shut off at some earlier time and the two men were there to turn it back on? Again, only they can tell us; and it might also cause us to contemplate as to whether the gas meter outside the building in the walled-off meter house was the 'large gas tank' of Sir Henry Buckland's imagination, which he wished us to believe was inside the Palace and very near to the spot where the fire started.

At the time of the fire, Mr. Stone formed his opinion that the fire was set, and has therefore come to the conclusion that it was arson, and always maintained this opinion. He is also of the opinion that somehow gas was used to trigger the fire, if only for the reason that gas, unlike most other incendiary devices, e.g. petroleum spirit, had a legitimate right to be in the building as an essential service, making it extremely difficult, if not impossible to prove whether an accidental leakage or a maliciously engineered one had occurred. Many other firemen at the scene share Mr. Stone's view as to arson, but differ on the question of triggering devices. On the other hand there are others, firemen included, who think of the fire as nothing more than an accidental, although spectacular, incident. One in particular is worthy of quote.

Sir Frederick Delve, C.B.E., a former and distinguished Chief Officer of the London Fire Brigade who, like Mr. Stone, responded magnificently to my repeated requests for assistance, answered my question about the possibility of arson by letter and wrote as follows: 'I do not recall at any time sabotage being advanced as the cause of the fire. The extent of the damage made it virtually impossible to discover with any degree of accuracy the actual cause but again, to the best of my recollection, from statements made by members of the staff defective wiring was the probable cause.'

Here we have two firemen, both professionals with a lifetime's experience behind them, with diametrically opposed views on the crucial question of whether it was an accident or arson. Mr. Stone remained, throughout his many years of service, just an ordinary fireman. Sir Frederick Delve achieved the highest rank in his profession, that of Chief Officer of the London Fire Brigade, with a string of formidable technical qualifications.

For the purpose of this book, and out of no disrespect for Sir Frederick Delve, the reader must ignore completely his elevated rank and his qualifications, for at the time of the Crystal Palace fire he was, in his own words, 'a relatively young Chief Officer.' His command at Croydon was also a relatively small one. The reader must therefore avoid falling into the trap of accrediting more importance to Sir Frederick's opinion because of rank, than to Mr. Stone's opinion because he never sought promotion and the rank which goes with it. Sir Frederick obviously was career-minded and ambitious where Mr. Stone was not and, as he has several times explained to the author, he joined the fire brigade because, in the uncertain years following World War One, the fire brigade offered security and a steady income.

Let us look closer at what Sir Frederick Delve has to say. He cannot recall sabotage being advanced as the cause of the fire. Doubtless, sabotage or arson are words which would not be uttered in his presence by his subordinates in the Croydon Fire Brigade: both are dangerous words, not to be bandied about without sound reason, because of their very serious criminal overtones. No responsible Chief Officer would permit himself or his men to indulge in idle gossip about something which could send people to prison for a long time.

To be sure, he is right when he says that the extent of the damage made it virtually impossible to discover with any degree of accuracy the actual cause of the fire. But his premise either overlooks or disregards something which, in all honesty, he may be unaware of but something which, if he is aware of it, most certainly should have aroused his suspicion and the suspicion of his superiors, particularly Major Morris in his capacity then of Chief Officer of the London Fire Brigade. Had the remains of the flooring of the Egyptian Court been subjected to chemical analysis, no matter how extensive the damage, the probability of arson would surely have been raised. In the light of two statements made by two different people who claim to have witnessed the fire in its formative stage, it is inconceivable that a chemical analysis was not insisted upon, unless some obscure conspiracy dictated that the true facts were not, at the time, in the public interest. But more of this later.

Sir Frederick concludes this part of his letter by referring to members of the Palace staff blaming defective electric wiring for the fire.

Before the advent of electricity, solid fuel fires using coal, wood and the like, faulty flues, candles, oil lamps, cigarettes and matches were the common scapegoats for outbreaks of fire, and they undoubtedly played their part in many large conflagrations, as well as in small fires. The Crystal Palace was the first public building to be installed with what has come to be seen as the greatest modern scapegoat for fire – electricity. Where evidence is either lacking or doubtful, an electrical defect is always put forward as the most probable cause. There can be no argument about the fire-raising potential of electricity cases of faulty or sub-standard installation or old, neglected poorly maintained circuits, (often overloaded by additional equipment not allowed for in the original specification).

On the other hand, where an electricity installation is correctly worked into a building and thereafter well and conscientiously maintained, a form of energy-producing heat and light exists which, for safety of operation, has no equal. The Crystal Palace was staffed by competent maintenance crews, plumbers, fitters, and electricians, and there is not a shred of evidence to suggest that things were neglected, either by incompetence or laziness. Under Sir Henry Buckland's ever-watchful and critical eye, anyone not completely on top of his job did not last long and was quickly out in the road hunting another job.

To return to Mr. Stone's observation of blowtorch-like flames moving horizontally as though being fed by gas or whatever; it will be recalled, that firemen made their way into the building and attempted to prevent fire spreading from the blazing centre transept into the north and south naves, and how they were driven out by flames of extraordinary length running high up under the roofs of both naves. It is feasible, therefore, that it was this phenomenon which Mr. Stone, was seeing; a phenomenon which fire engineers assert is particularly appropriate to structures of the Crystal Palace type with large, undivided open spaces, with high vault roofs and where the lengthy naves act like flues or horizontal chimneys drawing fire and hot gases into them with much force.

In order to put this theory to the test, I carried out a simple experiment using a model of the Palace. It was without any detail and somewhat crude, consisting of wire covered with transparent polythene, but accurate in as much as it truly represented a large centre transept with long naves running off it north and south, and with a slight but steady draught arranged to emanate roughly from a northerly direction, simulating the wind direction on the night of the fire. Both naves were left entirely empty of all material, but in the centre transept I placed a quantity of matchwood to represent the timber content of this part of the real building. The ends of both naves were flat cardboard cut to shape, not fastened, but just allowed to lean against the main structure.

Within fifteen seconds of ignition of the matchwood, and even before the roof of the centre transept had burned or melted through, there were clearly visible flames running beneath the transparent covering of the naves. The pressure of heat-expanded air quickly blew away the cardboard end wall of the south nave, and flame was streaming out of the open end before the roof had gone. The north nave was last to go, obviously by way of the direction of my simulated northerly wind. It is therefore almost a certainty that once a fire has gained a good hold on a centre transept, any naves running off it are doomed from the start, and the only way in which protection can be afforded against this would be the inclusion of a fire-stop wall at the intersection of transept and naves. If this is not practical, a further solution can be provided by the installation of deluge equipment designed to cover the entire arch of the naves at their intersection with the transept. The deluge system would consist of a high pressure main, perforated with sprinkler heads. In the event of fire a heavy water curtain would, by operation of the sprinkler heads, help considerably to blank off the naves from any fire in the transept.

Chief Officer Evans, then at London's Soho Fire Station and later at Beckenham, told the editor of the fire brigades journal Fire that he had never seen a fire spread so rapidly. 'Its progress could be seen by the reflected light.'

It is a sobering and disquieting thought that many of our great churches and irreplaceable cathedrals are built on the open nave transept plan, and would undoubtedly react, in the event of serious fire, as the Crystal Palace did. Fortunately, these architectural treasures are built of heavy stone and the inflammable contents confined to heavy hardwood, seating, and an organ – this being the most serious risk because of the flue-like behaviour of the organ pipes.

Besides gas and electricity, another popular theory for the cause the Crystal Palace fire is a supposed peculiarity in the laying down of the main floor. In the book 'The Phoenix Suburb' by Alan Warwick, which in the main deals with the history of Norwood and its adjacent districts, the assertion is made that Sir Joseph Paxton had the floor boards laid a quarter-inch apart, so that when the crowds had departed, the floors had only to be sprinkled and swept, and all the dust of the day would fall between the planks into the basement. Now if ever the old adage about sweeping dirt under the carpet was stretched to its ultimate, then this is it. One has only to contemplate the obnoxious smell which would arise out of the basement from decades of rotting food particles, sweets, chocolates, and discarded ice cream to appreciate the nonsense of this idea, to say nothing of the army of rats and other vermin which would thrive in such a muck heap. Warwick's theory is that as the years went by, the layer of dust below drew into a highly inflammable, even explosive mixture that required only to be ignited by a chance cigarette end, fanned by a draught to glow more strongly, and build up heat in the surrounding dust, thus starting the fire.

If Warwick's theory had any substance, the Crystal Palace would probably not have lasted twelve months, for if one equates the floor area to the area of quarter inch gaps, the odds are that in a matter of months hundreds of glowing cigarette ends would have dropped into the basement.

From a study of photographs where parts of the floor appear in the foreground, it is evident that there were gaps between the floor boards which may well have been in the region of a quarter of an inch. However, they are unlikely to have been put there for the easy disposal of dust, as Warwick asserts. Sir Joseph Paxton thought as an engineer, not as a rubbish disposal consultant. It is probably correct to assume therefore that he had the floor boards spaced apart as a bonus central heating system which would permit warm air generated by the boilers to rise upwards through the floor in winter, and cool air from basement draughts in summer.

So far as winter goes, and it accounts for approximately two thirds of the British climate, the greatest problem with the Crystal Palace was trying to keep it comfortably warm in cold weather; a problem which was never overcome, the building being notorious for its cold and draughts. Today, we are all familiar with large amounts of heat loss through glass hence, the cost of double-glazing – unheard of in Paxton's day – would have been prohibitive given the area of glass to be found in the Crystal Palace. Paxton had to make every possible use of the materials and methods at his disposal, hence the gaps in the floor. The existence of the gaps would allow dust and debris to fall into the basement, but basic hygiene would demand the clearing of the basement at frequent intervals. In 1936, the laws of hygiene in premises devoted to public assembly had become stricter than in Victorian times, and the maintenance of a reasonably clean basement at the Palace would be insisted upon.

It is to be admitted that, in so far as it goes, Warwick's theory about a glowing cigarette end starting fires in dust is admissible. Accumulations of dust are recognised today as being a serious fire hazard. There was no explosion of dust or otherwise at the Crystal Palace but, in view of Warwick's theory we shall briefly consider the phenomenon of a dust fire – a very different thing from a dust explosion, although in certain given circumstances or conditions both can become related.

It is now known that fire can commence in certain types of dust distributed in layers or heaps. Dusts in this category are timber sawdust, rubber dust, textile dust or fluff, and solid fuel dusts – coal, coke, and anthracite. There are others, but we must concern ourselves only with those likely to be present in the Palace basement, which would include all of those listed above. Over a prolonged period, the friction of rubber footwear on a timber floor will produce a very fine dust of both materials. The same will apply to clothing made from textiles. In a building frequented by millions of people over many years, a prodigious quantity of textile clothing will eventually find its way beneath the flooring. Solid fuel dusts, as listed above, would be present because of the nature of the central heating plant.

A glowing cigarette end will undoubtedly induce a smouldering fire on the surface of a dust heap or layer. If, however, a layer of dust of 2mm or more is deposited on a hot surface (the minimum depth varies according to the nature of the dust) a deep-seated, very slow smouldering can be propagated within the base of the layer or heap when the heat intake from the hot surface exceeds the heat dispersal to the surrounding air adjacent to the surface. A hot surface in this context could be a poorly insulated boiler casing, steam or hot water piping, overheated electrical circuits, or overheated machinery, e.g. electric motors or machine bearings.

This deep-seated smouldering will remain undetected; because it neither produces smoke or smell such as is usually associated with burning. The smell, if any, would be exceedingly slight and of a musty nature, as in a damp room. Depending on the depth of the layer, slow smouldering can continue over a very long period, running into weeks or even months, until it finally reaches the surface of the layer. Even at this stage, detection is difficult because the only outward sign would be a slight surface discoloration as ash is formed. Only with the sudden introduction of draught, or high oxygen content air, will visible glowing and flaming commence, sufficient to ignite adjacent combustibles.

Warwick's assertion overlooks several factors. First is the location of the first visible sign of fire – the ladies' cloakroom. Common decency alone would prohibit gaps in floorboards in a ladies' cloakroom. Secondly the Egyptian Court, where the first serious outbreak of fire from the cloakroom occurred, had a stone floor, although the entrance to it was of timber. The chances of a glowing cigarette end finding its way beneath the flooring of either the cloakroom or the Court, whilst not impossible, would be remote. Because both locations were close to Crystal Palace Parade and therefore at the highest point of the sloping ground, the basement at this point was comparatively shallow – no more than three or four feet. It is feasible therefore, that a dust fire could have commenced by contact with a heat agent and remained undetected for days, or weeks, until a chance draught produced flaming on the dust surface.

Another factor which not only Warwick but also the fire officers concerned appear to have missed, is a statement made to the Daily Mail by the late Sydney Legg, confidential private secretary to Sir Henry Buckland; this reads as follows: 'Shortly after 7:30pm, one of our firemen raced to my house to tell me that a fire had broken out in the Egyptian Hall. I found that part of the hall was ablaze, and a stream of flame was racing along the floor like a will-o-the-wisp.'

'The Palace's own firemen turned three hoses on it, but in what seemed no time the trail of flame had blazed into the centre transept. As soon as I saw that our own men could not cope with the outbreak, I telephoned for the fire brigade and for Sir Henry Buckland, who arrived within a few minutes. Sir Henry remained in the hall to superintend operations until the arrival of the brigades. Within fifteen minutes the whole interior was a mass of flames'.

So far as I have been able to discover by lengthy study of the national and provincial newspapers of the day, Mr. Legg's statement to the Daily Mail and its staff reporter Mr. Allan Rands is exclusive. It is also the most important by far to come to light, and in its brief but telling second sentence lies the key which throws open the door to the whole mystery. '...a stream of flame was racing along the floor like a will-o-the-wisp.'

Unfortunately, Mr. Legg died four years before research on this book began, so he is beyond questioning. We must assume that he knew the precise meaning of the term will-o-the-wisp, even though he may have failed to recognise its implication which, in a well-informed intelligent man, seems improbable. It may be that he was advised to ignore the implication and to refrain from repeating his account to any other news reporters, lest he blew the lid off a conspiracy considered not to be in the public interest.

Will-o-the-wisp is a term used to describe a strange phenomenon which takes the form of a pale, bluish flame seen over marshes during the hours of darkness, flickering and moving at great speed, and often referred to by country folk as a 'Jack-o-Lantern'. Its precise make up is not known with any degree of certainty, but is thought to be a combination of marsh gas and an electro-static discharge of comparatively low and harmless voltage, not to be confused with chain lightning which runs across open country in conditions of heavy thunder, with lethal voltage.

There was no marsh gas or thunder in the Egyptian Court of the Crystal Palace, therefore if Mr. Legg is to be believed, and if his observation was accurate, we have no alternative but to accept that some kind of inflammable effect was present in the Egyptian Court and, moreover, that its path lay across the Court and out through the open south portico, directly into the fire-prone wooden staging of the centre transept and its Great Orchestra. Nothing else can explain a stream of flame racing along a floor or any other surface.

'A streak of flame ran along the top of the room, and the place was ablaze in a moment.' This, as quoted previously, is Sir Henry Buckland's statement, a verbatim account of what he told a Palace fireman, probably Mr. Clark. No stronger confirmation for Mr. Legg's evidence could be found in any court of law. A stream of flame racing like a will-o-the-wisp and a streak of flame running along the top of the room are one and the same; only the wording is different and both effects are scientifically out of the question without the presence of an alcohol- or petroleum-based propellant.

There is no obvious or valid reason other than arson for the existence of a petroleum or alcohol base. There is no valid reason other than arson for the existence of such substance in such quantity on the floor of any building or structure, except in the case of accidental spillage in a workshop. Thus, it could be argued that the case for arson at the Crystal Palace is established beyond reasonable doubt. Nor is this the end of the story because the whole time factor, as given by Sir Henry Buckland and his staff, stands disputed by outside witnesses.

In response to my Daily Mirror appeal for assistance, I received a letter from a Mrs. M. Sullivan, of South Norwood. In 1936, Mrs. Sullivan was employed by the Telephone Manufacturing Co. Ltd., which became part of the Pye Telecommunications Group located in Martell Road, West Dulwich. She wrote as follows: 'At the time of the Crystal Palace fire, I was working at the Company. Normally we finished our day at 5:30pm. On this particular instance my colleague and I had worked overtime. In the usual way there would have been several of us going in the same direction earlier'.

'As near as I can remember we worked till 6:30pm, certainly no later. I was meeting my fiancée at 7:30pm.'

'As we had been sitting all day, we decided to walk, instead of waiting for the bus, as far as the Crystal Palace, and from here we would board a trolley bus for Norwood. However, as we walked along towards the Palace, we approached the Parade from a side turning opposite. It was then that we saw smoke, and could smell it. The walk from Martell Road would have taken between fifteen and twenty minutes; not more. In truth, I would say it was between 6:45pm, and 7:00pm, and the Palace was burning then with the flames spreading at an incredible speed.'

Conscious as I am of the tricks which lengthy time lapse can play with one's memory, I had no alternative but to question Mrs. Sullivan carefully on this question of time, and went so far as to suggest to her that her memory may have been at fault. She accepted this with good grace, but was adamant that such was not the case, and that the Palace was burning between the times quoted above; 6:45pm at the earliest and 7:00pm at the latest.

Mrs. Sullivan was also puzzled by the fact that there was no sign of any fire brigade, or any apparent action being taken by several bystanders who were watching the fire. This in itself is not unusual. The history of buildings lost for the reason that bystanders assume always that someone else has called the fire brigade, and so need not bother to do so themselves, is a lengthy and deplorable one. The critical question in this case is, why did Sir Henry Buckland and his staff not call the Penge Fire Brigade at 7:00pm, rather than 7:59pm if, as Mrs. Sullivan insists, a serious and rapidly spreading fire was under way at the earlier time?

It would indeed be easy to dismiss Mrs. Sullivan's story as a simple memory failure. I must admit that at first I was tempted along that line until further verification, particularly of her time factor, came quickly to hand. Before proceeding, let me explain that a test walk at moderate pace from Martell Road to Crystal Palace Parade proved to be easily accomplished in twenty minutes, exactly as Mrs. Sullivan recalls; at a brisk pace, the same distance can be covered in fifteen minutes.

Following close on Mrs. Sullivan's letter was one from a Mr. A. L. Bridges of Upper Norwood, whose sister-in-law worked at the Palace at the time of the fire. It is important to stress that although this lady worked in the Palace, she was not employed by Sir Henry Buckland or the Palace Trustees and, therefore, was completely beyond the influence of either. She was, in fact, in the direct employ of Mecca Catering Ltd. They had, at the time, a major catering concession at the Palace with a table-linen laundry situated in one of the maze of timber and galvanized out-buildings which were interspaced between the south transept and the south tower and which, as already related, caused much headache for the firemen trying to keep the fire from reaching the tower.

Mr. Bridge's sister-in-law worked in this laundry, and on the night of the fire she finished work and clocked out at 6:00pm precisely. To get out of the complex she had to walk the length of the south transept and nave to make good her exit by way of the main entrance in the centre transept. So far as she could see, everything was normal, with no sign of any fire; not even a hint of it either by way of smoke or smell. This lady had reached her home in Palace Square, and was in the act of changing and freshening up before sitting down to tea when, at 6:45pm by her bedroom clock, she noticed a red glow through her bedroom window. On looking out she could see, to quote her own words, '…that the Palace was on fire with the centre transept going up like a rocket.'

Here we have positive confirmation of Mrs. Sullivan's story with a narrowing of the time factor to a positive 6:45pm which is Mrs. Sullivan's earliest quote for her arrival on the Parade. Even allowing for some inaccuracy in a bedroom clock, Mr. Bridges' sister-in-law's evidence corroborates all that Mrs. Sullivan told me.

Mr. Bridges' sister-in-law along with many other local residents even now still hold fast to the opinion that the fire was set, as the quickest, also most efficient, and the cheapest way of bringing the Palace down – and a profitable way to boot, because of the insurance to be collected. Such opinions, while remaining in the realm of speculation, cannot be ignored, given the inescapably suspicious mountain of evidence resulting from my research; evidence which does not end with Mrs. Sullivan, or with Mr. Bridges' sister-in-law.

My next witness was Philip Manning who, in 1936, was working at Woolwich Arsenal and lived on Woodland Road, Gipsy Hill. His son Patrick wrote to me that on the 30th November 1936, his dad left the Arsenal as normal at about 5:00pm and bicycled to his home via Crystal Palace Parade. As he was passing the Palace north of the centre transept he could see a flame flickering just inside the building. He went to the Police Station at the junction of Gipsy Hill with Central Hill to report the matter, only to be told that workmen were working in the building that night using oxy-acetylene equipment. He went home, and just as he walked into his house called out, 'Maybe the Crystal Palace is on fire'. The family came out and saw that the Palace was indeed burning. All this happened between 7:00pm and 7:30pm.

During a round of correspondence with a George Bennison, Honorary Secretary of the London Fire Brigade Retired Members Association, I received a letter from him confirming to a certain extent the above comment. He states 'There was a strong rumour, current at the time, that maintenance staff had been carrying out certain work and that a small fire had actually occurred during the afternoon which had been dealt with at once and supposedly (his emphasis) extinguished without notifying the Brigade. This, I emphasise, was rumour, but it did carry some considerable weight at the time of the fire'.

My last witness was, in 1936, in the direct employ of Sir Henry Buckland and working in the Palace Park & Gardens Department.

On the night of the fire, Mr. S. Neale worked late, stoking the boilers in the greenhouses which contained all of the various plants used both in the Palace itself and in the gardens. He held his responsible post for twenty-two years. His statement reads as follows: 'After finishing my work, I made my way into the Crystal Palace building in order to punch my time card on the time clock which was in the firemen's quarters in the centre of the building. I punched my time card exactly on 7:00pm, and whilst doing so had a chat with one of the duty firemen. During the course of this a member of the public entered the building asking the fireman if there was a fire inside as from the road, there appeared to be a red glow inside the glass.

The fireman went to the place indicated by the man, and there was a small fire near a glass section. Immediately the fireman got the hose to work, and within two minutes the fire was out.'

Besides confirming the approximate time factor as being within the limits set by Mrs. Sullivan, Mr. Bridges' sister-in-law, and Mr. Manning, Mr. Neale's story raises several pointed questions. First, it would suggest the existence of two fires in different locations at different times. One fire just inside the glass and visible from outside at 7:00pm and a second, that discovered by Mr. Clark, at some time between 7:30pm and 7:40pm in the ladies' cloakroom. This was not visible from outside because between the cloakroom and the outer glass wall, there was both a passage, or narrow hall, and the main office section.

Any experienced fireman or fire investigator takes a very dim view indeed when he comes across two fires in different parts of the same building. This is especially so when there appears to be a time lag between the fires. Suspicion of arson is aroused immediately because the modus operandi of the typical fire-raiser is to set more than one fire on the assumption that if one fire fails to take hold, a second one will. If such was not the case, and we are dealing with only one of two fires, then the one which was thought to be out at 7:00pm was not put out as Mr. Neale thought and must have continued to burn unseen, probably beneath the flooring, only to reappear half an hour or so later in the ladies' cloakroom. If that was the case, then it was in curious neglect of his duty either through ignorance, an ignorance of the basic fundamentals of firemanship, sheer laziness, or because it was his predetermined intention to do no more than to appear to extinguish a fire of which he already had prior knowledge, and over which he had been caught out by the vigilance of a passer-by. If the latter were the case, then he was either the arsonist, or a party to an arson conspiracy. A correctly trained and conscientious fireman, having extinguished a visible fire, would follow through with a thorough check. This would take the form of a careful search on all four sides, as well as above and below the immediate and adjacent area of the fire, so as to make certain that no hidden burning was in progress. In the case of the Crystal Palace, the underside of the floor, i.e. the basement should, in particular, have been searched.

If we are to accept the evidence of the aforementioned witnesses, if we are to accept the times which they give and the time given by Mr. Neale – all within the space of 6:45-7:00pm – then there can be no escaping the fact that either there were two fires; the one which Mr. Neale saw put out, and a second already burning fiercely in the ladies' cloakroom, or was there one big fire raging in the basement and breaking upwards through the floor at two points, one just inside the glass as seen by several members of the public and Mr. Neale, and which had been thought to have been put out, and the other through the floor of the ladies' cloakroom?

Who was the fireman with whom Mr. Neale was chatting? If it was Mr. Clark, how was it that he could handle successfully a high-pressure hose unaided at 7:00pm, and yet be knocked over by a similar hose later when assisted by Mr. Tullett? All the fire hoses were under equal pressure and volume because they were all supplied with water from the same source and the same main. According to Mr. Neale it was not Mr. Clark. In answer to a letter asking if he could name the fireman to whom he was talking, and if it was Mr. Clark, he replied as follows, 'In reference to your enquiry as regards Mr. Clark being the fireman on duty at the time of the Crystal Palace fire being the man I was talking to, I can assure you he was not the fireman I spoke to. The reason why I am so sure is that I knew Mr. S. Clark as well as Mr. Tullett for quite a number of years.' The inference here is that whilst knowing Sydney Clark and Frank Tullett well, Mr. Neale did not know the fireman with whom he was in conversation.

As we have already seen, according to Sydney Clark's story to his wife he was alone, except for Frank Tullett who was not a fireman. It would, on that basis, appear that Mr. Neale was one of those on the day shift, and the fire which he tackled was spotted just before 7:00pm, at which time the shifts changed and Sydney Clark would take over for the night.

Unpalatable though it may be, we must now face the strong possibility that Sydney Clark's whole story is suspect, for it is almost certain that when he arrived for duty at 7:00pm the Crystal Palace was already sufficiently alight to be visible from outside. It follows from this, therefore, that if he in fact found himself with Frank Tullett as his sole companion, then he was the victim of a wholesale desertion by the three day-shift firemen. Whether or not this is what occurred, it would seem now pretty-well established that at least the part of Clark's story which tells of him discovering a fire between 7:30pm and 7:40pm is a fabrication engineered for the express purpose of making it appear that the delay over calling the fire brigade was much shorter than was really the case. The same must apply to Sir Henry Buckland and all the others who give those times for the discovery of the fire. It is inconceivable that Sydney Clark would fabricate an untruth of this nature on his own initiative, because he was only an employee and not responsible for policy-making. The initiative would spring from his superiors, and he would have been told what to say by them. It would not be difficult to see the mind of Sir Henry Buckland behind this, although we cannot be certain of it, and it matters little, for at best it can be described only as a ramshackle attempt at covering up what otherwise would have been an impossible position in trying to satisfactorily explain away at least an hour's delay, if not an hour and a quarter, in calling the fire brigade. What stuns the senses, and defies all credibility is the arrogance behind the fabrication. To assume that it would be believed, and never be contested, points to the perpetrator or perpetrators as having a total and cynical disregard for the intelligence of others.

If the first part of Sydney Clark's story is untrue, then so must be the second part, for if the Palace was seriously on fire when he arrived for duty at 7:00pm he could not, by any stretch of the imagination, have been knocked over by a fire hose while trying to subdue a fire confined to the ladies' cloakroom at 7:30-7:40pm. How, then, did his dentures and his spectacles come to be broken? When one thinks about it sufficiently, if a man equipped with spectacles and dentures were to be thrown over by a live fire hose, then his spectacles would probably be thrown off and broken either by contact with the ground, or by being trodden on in the resulting confusion. His dentures however would be another matter. By reason of their function, dentures are made very strong so that they may resist several forces exerted upon them continuously while in the mouth; those forces include compression, bending, twisting and stretching. If correctly fitted they also bed down onto the gums and in the case of the upper plate are held fast on the roof of the mouth by suction which has to be released before the plate can be removed. It is unlikely that dentures would become dislodged and ejected from the mouth as the result of a fall such as would stem from the knock-over effect of an uncontrolled fire hose. The only way that the dentures would fall out or break would be if the victim were to be struck in the face by the heavy gunmetal branch pipe and nozzle, in which case serious facial injury would be unavoidable. Sydney Clark suffered no facial injury to speak of, and to check this out I contacted his wife yet again. She was either not conscious of her husband having received facial injury, or declined to comment on it. She did say however that until the morning after the fire she had never seen her husband cry. Between sobs, he said repeatedly, 'I did try to save it; I did try to save it.'

There can be little doubt that Sydney Clark was a deeply conscientious man devoted to the ideal of doing a job well in so far as circumstances and his training would allow; whether or not his version of the facts as to what happened as related to his wife is true or false can never detract from this. Could it be that what actually took place went something like this – Sydney Clark arrived for work at some time just before 7:00pm and found the Palace to be on fire. He then tried very hard to enter the building to see what he could do, but was forcibly prevented from doing so because of the danger to his life, because there were things which he was not supposed to see, or a combination of both, and that his dentures and spectacles were broken as the result of a struggle to deny him entry to the building. If that were the case, it would seem that events prior to Clark's arrival might have gone as follows. Somewhere between 6:30pm and 7:00pm a fire was ignited by persons unknown inside the glass wall of the centre transept, close to the back of the Great Organ and the underside of the timber staging of the Great Orchestra – the most readily combustible part of the whole complex, (this would have been the fire spoken of by Mr. Neale), the successful growth of which was prevented by the intervention of a passer-by who, seeing the red glow from outside, entered the building to report what he had observed to the duty fireman who was talking to Mr. Neale. Foiled by the passer-by and his vigilance, the arsonist or arsonists then proceeded to the ladies' cloakroom, which they knew by the nature of its usage to be well shielded from outside view. In the cloakroom a second fire was set, and a trail of low flash-point, petroleum-based spirit laid down across the floor of the Egyptian Court and out through one of the open south porticos straight into the centre transept and the dried out timber of the Great orchestra; Mr. Legg's 'will-o-the-wisp' flames racing across the floor exactly as he related to Allan Rands of the Daily Mail.

Further support for the earlier time factor, i.e. those given by the witnesses, comes from a Mr. Ford, late of Southend-on-Sea, who at the time of the fire was a newspaper reporter having a coffee in a café opposite the main entrance to the Palace on the Parade. Mr. Ford told this writer that he left the café at approximately 6:55pm to find the centre part of the Palace illuminated by flames.

Two graphic and vivid accounts of the fire as seen from inside the building have been left to us by Miss Roper-Norrish, a violinist in the orchestra and Mr. A. Talbot, a clerk in the Palace general office from before the 1914-18 war.

Miss Roper-Norrish said to newsmen after the fire, 'I had barely time to gather up some money that was the property of the orchestra and run for it to the exit. Already the flames were blazing terrifyingly in the centre transept, where there were piles of chairs. The Handel Organ was near the flames and from it were coming the most strange groans, like some person in terrible pain. It was afterwards said that the sound was produced by violent heat forcing air through the organ pipes. But I shall never forget those ghastly groans.'

Mr. A. Talbot told the News Chronicle newspaper, 'The fire started in the centre section. I saw the whole thing. Inside the Palace the tiers of wooden seats and supports used in the concerts blazed like matchwood. The steel frame bent and cracked in the furnace. Panes of glass in the roof, measuring 30inches by 40inches and weighing as much as a man. buckled and melted in streams of molten glass.'

Here, then, the case either for accident or for arson must rest. The result is far from satisfactory, far from conclusive; and so it must be, for much of the evidence is unsatisfactory and inconclusive. The affair happened so long ago and, because of this, far too many of those who may have been able to add vital pieces to the puzzle are dead, have memories dimmed by age or, even after all these long years, are still afraid to come forward. So we must make the best of what we have. It is this writer's opinion that what evidence we have points strongly to a set fire: a work of arson. It is therefore important to conclude with a further short chapter in which we will look at possible motives, and also discover the identity of two people who knew before the event that the Crystal Palace was to be destroyed.

Chapter six

Motive

The reasons which motivate the fire-raiser or arsonist are many and varied. The motivation is nearly always criminal, and can be listed under the following four headings: (1) intent to defraud; (2) pyromania; (3) intent to cover up or destroy evidence of a crime; (4) senseless vandalism – a somewhat modern phenomenon not widely experienced before the Second World War.

Above we have the most common motives and all of them criminal insofar as the law is concerned. However, there is a fifth – political motivation. We must also include in this fifth circumstance acts of revenge, wherein individuals or even whole nations are set against one another to destroy their respective properties and/or wealth. Let us attempt now to apply those five motivations to the Crystal Palace fire and see which, if any, fits the case.

Intent to defraud

It is popular belief that the Crystal Palace was failing financially, and that in order to correct this it was decided to burn down the building so as to claim the insurance. The idea undoubtedly grew root because in 1933 a Mr. Leopold Harris, the head of a firm of fire assessors, was brought to trial and convicted for a series of massive fire insurance frauds which badly shook both the insurance and the banking world. Harris received a 14-year prison sentence, and because of the widespread publicity given to the case the public at large tended to look at every large fire as a possible repeat of the Harris affair. So far as the Crystal Palace was concerned there was also a certain ignorance, or at least some misconception, about who actually owned it and how it was to be judged a financial success or failure.

As we have already seen, the Crystal Palace ceased to be a privately-owned profit-making enterprise in 1909, when the Crystal Palace Company was wound up in the bankruptcy court. Again, as we have already seen, the building was saved by financial donations from individuals (in particular, Lord Plymouth) and institutions. From that point, on the Palace became the property of the Nation. To secure and protect the Nation's acquisition required the setting up of a Charitable Trust representing the City of London and the several local government authorities, mainly those whose sphere of influence bordered upon the Palace. The practical day-to-day running of the complex was left to the new General Manager, Henry Buckland and his staff.

His brief required him to make the Palace self-supporting in so far as he should keep it free of any requirement for a rate subsidy, and in this he was successful (as he had been with Harrogate Spa). The years before 1936 were devoted to a large extent to the work of restoring the building and the grounds. This mammoth task involved the ploughing back of almost all the income apart from day-to-day running costs. It stands greatly to Sir Henry's credit that he succeeded magnificently with both the restoration and in using the restored sections as each became available, to attract the public through the turnstiles in ever-increasing numbers. As a reward for this superhuman effort he was knighted in 1931. The income for the year 1934-1935 added up, in round figures, to £52,541, with an expenditure of £52,692, a debit balance of £542. Sir Henry was sailing very close to the wind – close enough for his worries and anxieties to have been enormous. To have suffered such a burden while maintaining a buoyant, cheery self-optimism throughout, points only to a very brave and courageous man. Burdened with pressure he was, nevertheless, almost succeeding in his task and had, moreover, reached the point where he could look forward with confidence to better times, for the expenditure on restoration was about at an end. So by no stretch of the imagination was he in the position where an insurance fire was appropriate, and because of the unsatisfactory state of the Palace itself such a course, even had it succeeded, would have amounted to financial lunacy.

To have started from the ground up, it is estimated that in terms of 1936 costs it would have required some four to five million pounds to rebuild the Crystal Palace. Set against such sums of money, the amount to be gained from a total loss insurance claim was pathetic and would hardly have covered design work and laying of new foundations. The building itself was insured by a first loss policy of £110,000 and placed with Lloyds underwriters. The concert organ was separately insured for £10,000, while other insurances (Mecca Cafés, Baird Television and the Badminton Club) amounted to another £88,000, making a total insurance value of £198,000. Thus, the whole concept of an insurance fire on a premises so grossly under-insured can be dismissed as a nonsense. So, too, can the idea still prevalent among some people that Sir Henry Buckland himself fired the Palace in order to purloin the insurance money for his own personal gain. In the first place he had to account for every penny to the trustees and secondly, such a suggestion is a cruel, iniquitous and monstrous libel against a man who devoted a large part of his life to the Palace which he loved, and strove always to improve, just as Sir Joseph Paxton had done before him.

Mr. John Henderson, manager of the Park, spoke to me at length on his close working relationship with Sir Henry Buckland in the years after the Second World War. On the subject of the insurance money, Mr. Henderson asserts that Sir Henry guarded and nurtured the money to the extent that he refused to sanction any expenditure even for the maintenance of machine tools and other equipment in the Palace workshop. This parsimony even extended to a Palace service motor truck running on the road with expired licence and tax fees, so determined was Sir Henry to save every penny for the purpose.

Pyromania

Unlike the fire insurance swindler, the pyromaniac is not motivated by personal material gain. Rather, he is a mentally unbalanced, often frustrated personality, fascinated by fire itself and the high drama of flaming destruction and gleaming red fire engines associated with it. Once having started his fire, it is usual for him to hang around watching the result of his handywork. His targets are mostly unoccupied premises so as to avoid the chance detection. For that reason, and so far as the Crystal Palace is concerned, we can count him out, although to protect such a huge building would require many guards.

Intent to cover up or destroy evidence of a crime

This reason can be dismissed as having no relevance to our case. No known serious crime took place at the Crystal Palace. Much petty crime must have taken place there over the years, but to destroy the building to cover up such a crime would be pointless.

Vandalism

Even today this crime remains relatively petty, and does not usually involve arson on a large scale. In the years before the Second World War, vandalism by present-day standards was non-existent. If the Crystal Palace remained standing today, the vandal would probably be content to throw stones at the glass.

Personal revenge and political motivation

We shall deal first with personal revenge. We already know that Sir Henry was, if judged by present-day standards a hard, no-nonsense employer, quick to pay off any employee who in his view was a slacker or disloyal. It is impossible to tell if an employee was so dismissed just prior to the fire, because all records relating to the staff were either destroyed by the fire or lost over the years in one way or another. Mr. Henderson's association with Sir Henry Buckland began in 1949, at which time he gave up a good position in the north of England to come and work at the Crystal Palace; at the time there were good reasons for believing that the Palace would be rebuilt, and therefore offer a promising future for someone wishing to better himself. Because Mr. Henderson was not at the Palace before the War, he could only repeat to the author what he had been told by old employees, those with whom he had talked about the old days before the fire, and for which there is no proof. Mr. Henderson claims to have been told that Sir Henry Buckland had several narrow escapes from serious injury, or worse, when heavy tools had a habit of falling from the roof close to where he happened to be walking or standing. If indeed such a thing did occur from time to time, it would be impossible to prove that the tools were dropped with intent to cause injury. What is well known, however, is that such action is a favourite and often successful method of getting rid of someone who is disliked. Sir Henry Buckland was by nature far too self-assured to be frightened by such ruses, so it might follow that if sufficient antagonism had grown up over a period, then someone having failed to frighten or even kill Sir Henry may have decided on the alternative of destroying his life's work, and so to fire the building.

Rumour and speculation are, even to this day, so rife about Sir Henry that one is continually at a loss to tell fact from fiction. For instance, three different people, all living in Sydenham, one of whom was closely related to a woman who had run a fairground in the Palace grounds for many years, claimed that Sir Henry had become mixed up with British Nazi sympathisers. They thought that he fired the Palace as a beacon, or signal for the commencement of a right wing putsch to overthrow the government of the day and establish totalitarian rule in this country, taking his cue from the alleged Nazi burning of the Reichstag in Berlin. This to me smacked of being a tall story, and when I put it to Mr. Henderson he was emphatic that from his lengthy relationship with Sir Henry he was certain that politics played no significant part in his life, and that any suggestion to the effect that he had become involved with the Nazis was absurd. Mr. Henderson did tell me, however, that after the war Sir Henry did develop the habit of frequently taking himself off to the House of Commons, sometimes for days on end. On the face of it, such behaviour would suggest a more than casual interest in politics, but the facts of the matter are that his interest was limited to lobbying MPs to rebuild the Crystal Palace to house the Festival of Britain; a forlorn hope as things turned out, for the Festival went to the much-publicised and overrated South Bank of the Thames.

Several tales were related to me about Sir Henry Buckland which are too bizarre for repetition here. One, however, because it was given first hand by Lady Buckland, does deserve mention. Lady Buckland told the author that although travel abroad was severely restricted during the war years for other than leading statesmen and service personnel, her husband was, on occasion, given a permit to travel for the express purpose of viewing up-to-date entertainment complexes in countries which either belonged the Allied cause, or were friendly to it; this so as to determine what, if any, modern ideas might be put to good account in a rebuilt Crystal Palace. One of these trips turned out to be somewhat prolonged, with Sir Henry being absent from home for a lengthy period. Suddenly, it dawned on Lady Buckland that she was being shunned and ignored in the street by people whom she knew, and counted as friends. At a loss to account for this strange behaviour, and much hurt by it, she decided to make discreet enquiries, only to discover to her horror that it was commonly believed that her husband was being held in prison as a suspected German spy. To kill this belief required legal pressure on certain persons reputed to have given birth to the story.

There is an old saying, 'there is no smoke without fire'. If this were applied to Sir Henry, one might reasonably assume that the rumours pointing to his possible connection with a circle of Nazi sympathisers were fact. However, the author has been unable to uncover one scrap of worthwhile evidence supporting this theory, and so considers it very likely that the story evolved from Lady Buckland's wartime experience having been given a particularly nasty twist.

Having come so far in the hope that some, at least, of the absurdities surrounding the person of Sir Henry Buckland have been put to rest, and having dealt with personal revenge and touched upon politics, it remains only for us to examine the last remaining political motivation which can possibly have any real bearing on the Crystal Palace fire.

London had a population of seven and a half million people in 1936, all undefended, whilst across the English Channel Adolf Hitler was in the process of building the greatest air force of all time. Away to the southeast of London and within a few miles of the heart of the British Empire was the huge bulk of the Crystal Palace, crowning the heights of Sydenham and visible from many miles distant. Even when the capital itself was hidden in fog, the Crystal Palace would stand out like some giant's signpost suspended in the air, pointing the way to the heart of the world's greatest city. On a moonlit night the Palace, with its acres of glass, shone like a vast mirror, one third of a mile in length, and to airline captains approaching Croydon airport it was a friendly and reassuring beacon, much in the same way as a lighthouse is to a sea captain. If the Palace was a reassuring sight to airline captains coming in for a landing at a friendly airport, then to a German bomber pilot approaching a blacked-out London, a hostile enemy city, the Crystal Palace would have appeared as a gift from heaven, verifying with exceptional clarity and accuracy the bomber's position in relation to its target.

The air was already heavy with menace when, on the afternoon of Monday 30th November 1936, Mr. W. B. Flowers of Clapham, along with his brother, walked into an off-licence at 43 Dorset Road south Lambeth, tobe told by the proprietor, Alfred Baylis, that the Crystal Palace was due to burn to the ground that very night. Mr. Flowers was kind enough to outline his strange experience in a letter to me, the text of which appears below.

Dear Mr. Knowles,

I have just read a letter from you in the Mirror re the Crystal Palace fire. It brought back memories which I will relate. On the afternoon before the fire a Mr. Baylis of Dorset Road, Vauxhall, south Lambeth, off licence said to my brother and I, 'Are you going to the Crystal Palace fire tonight?' He said that he was not joking, so my brother took me with him on his motor bike. When we got there, everything was normal with little traffic about and not a sign of a fire, so we went in a café opposite the Palace to have a cup of tea before we went home. When we were leaving the café, the man behind the counter said, 'I have never seen the Palace lit up like that before.' When we looked across it seemed to be lit up right along the front, and for quite a time it got brighter. But we thought, how can it be a fire, as no fire engines were about until much later on. I knew as an ex-fireman that they could be there in minutes if they had been called. Another thing was that the Palace had their own fire service, and plenty of water from the tanks atop the two towers, and any fire could have been put down in minutes if need be.

I thought I would write as I feel sure that what I have said may interest you in some way, because it always seems to me that the Palace was meant to burn down, as I was told it was running into debt. But I cannot say myself if this was the case. I know we did not get home till the early hours as thousands of cars blocked our way.

Yours sincerely,
W. B. Flowers.

Obviously, it was of paramount importance to find Mr. Baylis if he was still alive, but in this we were unlucky, able only to trace his daughter who informed us that her father was dead, and that she was only ten years old at the time of the fire, and therefore unable to remember anything which her father may have said about it. This was a cruel blow, for if Mr. Flowers' story is true, then Mr. Baylis was either a prophet extraordinary, or he was party to a fire-raising conspiracy, if not actually involved in it, and so a witness of incalculable value to the solving of the Crystal Palace mystery.

There is no valid reason for doubting the honesty and integrity of W. B. Flowers, who consistently sticks to his story. We can accept or reject it. To reject it out of hand is like the ostrich with its head in the sand, whilst on the other hand, to accept such a tale without some sort of corroboration must almost certainly involve wishful thinking on the part of one keen to prove arson. The fact of the matter is, however, that corroboration of a sort, albeit indirect, does exist.

Mr. Geoffrey Gale, at the time of the Crystal Palace fire, was a Fleet Street proof-reader. But, of more importance to us, he was a lover of the organ as a musical instrument and is still, today, an organist of considerable repute. Moreover, he kept a diary in which he recorded his day-to-day experiences. On the Saturday immediately before the fire, he visited Crystal Palace for the purpose of trying his skill on the Great Handel Organ in the centre transept, arrangements for the visit having been made beforehand with Walter W. Hedgecock, who was at the time the official organist to the Palace. During the course of Geoff's visit a conversation ensued. Walter told him that he might never have the opportunity of either playing or hearing the Great Organ again. Geoff was taken aback, and his curiosity aroused by Walter's words which, if nothing else seemed extremely pessimistic. Determined not to let the matter rest there he asked Walter to explain himself. To this he replied, 'We will all know the answer to that before the end of the year, and possibly sooner. There is a war coming you know.' Geoff entered the details of the conversation in his diary, on the yellowed pages of which they remain to this day.

On the following Monday, Geoff attended an evening organ concert at Alexandra Palace, north London, during the course of which he was called outside onto the terrace to see, away to the south, the lurid glow in the sky over southeast London. The glow was the visible agony of the Crystal Palace burning. Just as Walter Hedgecock had intimated, less than three days earlier, that neither he nor anyone else would ever hear the Great Organ again. Before his eyes, as he stood sad and with heavy heart on the terrace of Alexandra Palace, the Crystal Palace and the Great Organ was being reduced to blackened ash and molten metal.

Undoubtedly, there will be those who will see, in Walter's words to Geoff, a reference only to the possibility of the Crystal Palace being destroyed, or at least being seriously damaged by bombing in the event of war. The idea, however, will not hold water because, in a descriptive booklet which he wrote about the Palace, Sir Henry tells how after the First World War, German Zeppelin and Gotha captains visiting the 1920 Palace War Exhibition told him that they were under very strict orders not to bomb the Palace. This was because of its great value as a landmark and verification as to their precise position in relation to London. In fact it is a matter of record that the nearest bombs fell in Beckenham.

In 1936, aviation, in spite of improved navigational aids, was still very dependent on ground sightings of prominent landmarks. A study of the Royal Air Force bomber offensive against Germany during the early years of the Second World War gives adequate evidence of this. Only much later, and towards the closing stages of the war, were air forces equipped with sophisticated, new electronic navigational aids, allowing for both the accurate location and the bombing of specific targets masked by cloud or fog.

Chapter seven

Postscript

When we consider the person of Sir Henry Buckland and the rumours, speculations, and legends which surrounded him in life, and continue to pursue him in death, then this book would be incomplete if it were to avoid the question as to whether or not he was involved in, or knew of an arson plot at the Crystal Palace.

As already shown, there are still many people in Sydenham, and the districts near it who are only too ready to describe Sir Henry Buckland as being a sinister shadowy figure, who used the Crystal Palace as a means of enriching himself, and dishonestly lining his own pockets – to the extent that, in the end, he fired the building for the purpose of obtaining for himself the insurance money payable on a total loss.

We have already seen, for clear-cut reasons, the insurance swindle theory to be so unlikely that it can be discounted. We have traced the career of Sir Henry from shop assistant to general manager of Harrogate Spa, then to general manager of the Crystal Palace, and finally to a Knight of the Realm; an overall achievement which could be attained only by a man with an outstanding determination to succeed and an unusual ability to both influence, and exert his authority on others. We have seen him to be arrogant and high-handed in his dealings with others, and somewhat tyrannical towards his employees, at least by today's standards although, at the same time, he could be extremely kind and generous to those employees whom he liked and who, for one reason or another fell into financial difficulty. Above all he was a master showman, a super-optimist and an opportunist; devious, cunning, and without many scruples when it came to making a quick pound for his beloved Crystal Palace. We know that he was disliked, even detested by many who knew him, and therefore had many enemies. In spite of stories to the contrary, we have no evidence that he was ever disloyal to his country or was anything other than a patriot. We have also seen how, when he took over responsibility for the Crystal Palace, he inherited what was virtually a mountain of broken glass, rusting iron, and rotting timber which gradually, over many years and as money which was earned not borrowed became available, he had restored to it to its original glory He introduced many improvements, the most important being the 'puttyless' reglazing of the roofs, and the rebuilding of the Great Organ in the centre transept. No man in his right mind burns down what accounted for the greater part of his life's work unless he were to be confronted by a set of exceptional circumstances which were at the time seemingly valid. Sir Henry could have been approached by some agency of government, or by some person or group of sufficient importance to command respect by those in high places who had become convinced that no lasting deal with Herr Hitler was possible, and that therefore war with Germany was inevitable. The problem of how best to protect London from air attack would then be close to the hearts of such people, and uppermost in their thinking. Once approached, and having become convinced of the value of the Crystal Palace as a target marker for the German bomber raids on London, Sir Henry may well have agreed to its removal as an essential to the security of London. If this were the case he seemingly confided to someone, for how else did the Mr. Baylis, proprietor of the south Lambeth wine store, know that the fire was due to break out in the evening of the very day that he spoke of, and forecast the fire to Mr. Flowers and his brother? How else was the chief organist at the Palace, Walter W. Hedgecock, in a position to tell Geoff Gale that he might never have the opportunity of seeing or hearing the Great Organ again? 'We will know the answer to that before the end of the year, and possibly sooner… There is a war coming you know'.

In the face of the above, it would be incredible, almost impossible, for Sir Henry to have been kept in the dark about what was to happen.

On the evening of Monday 30th November 1936 Sir Henry Buckland, on his own admission, left his house using, it would seem, a letter which required posting as reason for his going out. It is difficult, if not impossible to fix a time for his leaving home, because evidence as to the time of the fire's outbreak varies so widely. But whatever the time, it would appear to have been pre-arranged between Sir Henry and the fire raiser. The time would have been so fixed to allow for Sir Henry to arrive at the Palace a minute or so after the fire was lit when, as he told the press, 'I could see a red glow behind the office section, and immediately thought of fire. I rushed to the building at once.'

When Sir Henry left his house, he made sure to take his teenage daughter Chrystal with him. She, unknowingly had her part to play in the drama, for it must be assumed that she was intended to see the small fire in the ladies' cloakroom, and also to vouch for her father being at home at the time of the fire's origin. What she was not intended to see was the means by which the small fire was, in the course of four or five minutes, to break forth and engulf the whole of the great centre transept. Hence, to get his daughter out of the way, he told her to go to the Garden Hall far from the fire, and away in the south transept, to warn the rehearsing orchestra of a small fire. This she honestly believed from what she had seen with her own eyes and had been told by her father, was controllable and of no danger whatsoever. If in fact this had been the truth, it would in no way have been necessary to alarm the orchestra by sending a girl on such a fool's errand. On large ocean liners, in large hotels, hospitals and the like, small fires have often broken out and been extinguished without passengers, guests, or patients ever knowing about them. The cardinal rule is always to avoid alarming occupants, and other passengers unless a serious and potentially dangerous situation develops wherein life may be at risk. Chrystal Buckland was seemingly sent by her father to the south transept for one reason, and for no other – to prevent her seeing the trail of inflammable substance being set down on the floor of the Egyptian Court from a point just outside the ladies' cloakroom, then across the Court and out into the tinder dry contents of the great centre transept with its timber staging and thousands of wooden framed chairs.

It was this trail of inflammable liquid which appeared to Mr. Sydney Legg, as '…a stream of flame racing along the floor like a will-o-the-wisp'.

Only on leaving the Garden Hall, having carried out her father's instructions, did she re-enter the south nave to see, to her horror and dismay, a mass of flame raging out of control across the centre transept and already entering the south nave high up under the roof. 'Never, to this day,' she told me, 'have I been able to understand how, in the short space of four or five minutes, such a small fire grew to such gigantic and terrifying proportions.'

The terrifying rapidity with which the fire spread puzzled Chrystal Buckland because, being on her way to the Garden Hall, she was unable to see the trail of inflammable substance being set down on the floor of the Egyptian Court. We must at all times bear in mind that Sir Henry Buckland himself, in a statement quoted in Fire the highly respected professional journal of the British fire service, and dated for January 1937, which Sir Henry attributed to one of the Palace firemen reads as follows. 'A streak of flame ran along the top of the room, and the place was ablaze in a moment. The time was 7:25pm. I thought at first that gas was the cause; now we know,' says Sir Henry. There are many substances, such as alcohols, aldehydes, oils, acids, and even waxes today freely available to the public which, when in contact with air, give off heavy vapour, invisible and lying just above floor level. If ignited this could behave like a flashing will-o-the-wisp, flickering and dancing close to the floor. The point at issue, of course, is that few of these substances were accessible in the 1930s. Even if we were to allow for their existence, only relatively massive quantities of the substances would produce the result for which we are looking, and few would have any reason for being present in the Crystal Palace.

We are now left with one remaining question. Why was it that Sir Henry was seemingly present within a few minutes of the fire commencing? If Sir Henry had any hand in the fire he would have taken himself off to his club, the theatre, or anywhere that would put him many miles from Sydenham. Was Sir Henry Buckland in the Palace that night to make sure that the job of setting the fire was not bungled and also to be sure, in the event of anything going wrong, that he was there to take the blame and the full responsibility? Such was the measure of one man's courage and fearlessness, a characteristic which shone forth throughout his life and not one to be diminished by his by his failings.

It is this writer's firm conviction that he was badly let down, even betrayed by those government or private individuals who wanted the Crystal Palace removed. It is certain that being a shrewd and clever opportunist Sir Henry would seek to gain from the destruction of the Palace. He would in all probability, settle for no less than a guarantee from the conspirators that the Palace would be rebuilt if, or when the international climate improved or, if it came to the worst with war as the result, after it was over. The fact that Sir Henry nurtured and guarded the insurance money against the day when his dream of a new Palace could be realised; the fact that he had the ruined basement of the old building filled in with heavy rubble brought from London's bombed buildings, so as to create a level foundation for the new building, the fact that shortly after the war ended, he had new gas, electricity, and water mains laid onto the site is sufficient proof that he had very good reason for believing that his new Palace would be built.

The ultimate betrayal, one could even go so far as to call it the ultimate destruction of Sir Henry Buckland, came on the 3rd May 1951, when the Festival of Britain opened on the South Bank of the River Thames, in the centre of London. The Festival was part exhibition, part fun fair and entertainment complex, conceived and aimed at convincing the world that Britain still had enormous potential, even though exhausted and impoverished by war. The Festival itself was a temporary structure (just as Sir Joseph Paxton's original Crystal Palace had been when in Hyde Park for the Great Exhibition) but as a legitimate extension of the Festival, a permanent and massive structure was erected nearby to be called the Royal Festival Hall. Sir Henry Buckland believed that this should have found its rightful home at Crystal Palace, where a ready-made and perfectly situated site was ready and waiting for the builders to arrive. As it turned out, the builders have still to show up at Crystal Palace. However, two very important figures of the time did show up at Crystal Palace to examine the site, before finally deciding where the Festival of Britain was to be located. The figures were two politicians, Herbert Morrison MP, Deputy Prime Minister in the Attlee Labour government, and Hugh Gaitskell MP, both of whom were shown over the entire Crystal Palace site and grounds by Sir Henry Buckland, and his deputy and eventual successor, Mr. John Henderson. As it transpired, the Crystal Palace site was turned down out of hand by Morrison and Gaitskell, on the excuse that it was too far out of London and poorly served by public transport.

According to Mr. Henderson, it was Morrison who rather than Gaitskell who was the instigator of the stratagem above for ridding themselves of Buckland and the whole Crystal Palace controversy. Morrison was described to this writer by Mr. Henderson and by Mr. Stone, retired from Penge fire brigade, as an arrogant and unpleasant man. According to Mr. Henderson he showed neither interest in, nor a spark of enthusiasm for the Palace site, ignoring all Sir Henry said to him, and turning a blind eye to all he was shown. His general manner was both pompous and arrogant, and his rudeness to both Sir Henry and Mr. Henderson bordered on the unbearable. Lady Buckland told me that Mr. Henderson's assessment of Morrison was in line with her own and Sir Henry's impressions at the time. She also went on to tell me that it was rumoured that Morrison held a financial interest centred on old property on London's South Bank, and therefore stood to gain financially by pushing the South Bank site, as it would be necessary to purchase Morrison's land to make way for the Festival complex. However that may be, those responsible for organising the festival seem to have been persuaded by Morrison into turning their backs on the Sydenham venue and going all out for the South Bank site. I am sure that Lord Morrison had the rebirth and outstanding improvement of this neglected area of London very much at heart when he turned his eyes away from Sydenham. It must also be remembered that at the time of the decision to develop the South Bank as London's national cultural centre, the Crystal Palace site was still just outside the London County border. When referring to the Crystal Palace site, it essential not to confuse this piece of land with the sports complex and stadium which stands on ground below the site of the original Palace.

October 1976 saw the last Motor Show in London and in October 1977 the event transferred to the new centre in Birmingham and will, without doubt, he followed there by every other major exhibition held in this country. Sir Henry Buckland's design for a new Palace proposed at least three huge halls, each separate from the other, and similar in concept to what has in fact taken place in Birmingham, although this is of course almost double the area. But it proves Sir Henry to have been a man of sound vision, and his three hall proposal for Sydenham would have left ample room for further expansion if such were desirable.

Lady Buckland and her daughters Chrystal and Irene told me that losing the Festival was the end of the road for Sir Henry and the Crystal Palace, and from that point on he simply lost heart and interest in what he came to regard as a lost cause. He went to his grave still insisting that gas was the cause of the Crystal Palace fire and, so far as I have been able to learn from the Buckland family, he never at any time hinted at or referred to any other possibility. When questioned on the day after the fire by the *Daily Telegraph* Special

84

Correspondent as to the feasibility of sabotage or arson, Sir Henry replied: 'No suspicion of the kind was entertained.' 'Such a thing,' he added, 'is impossible.'

Sir Henry Buckland was too intelligent a man ever to believe in the impossibility of anything. His statement was designed to kill stone dead, and put a final stop to speculation on those lines.

It could be said with truth, that the Reichstag in Berlin was the first structural and architectural victim of the Second World War. I believe it to be true that the Crystal Palace was the second structural and architectural victim of that war.

In a speech given to a gathering of people interested in the Palace at London's Guildhall on January 29th 1937, Sir Henry Buckland had this to say: 'In a world of rapid movement and change the Crystal Palace was, in a sense, a spiritual city set on a hill. It represented the idealism of eighty-five years ago, and while much of that idealism has perished in the floods of change with comparatively few of its objectives gained, yet some part of it has survived, and to its survival the Palace was a witness.'

Kirk's Law

Because of Sir Henry Buckland's insistence that gas was the cause of the fire, this required careful consideration and evaluation. Paul L. Kirk is one of the world's most respected fire investigators. In his book 'Fire Investigation' he tells us that for fire to propagate, a ratio of one in ten must be achieved. 'One volume of town gas to ten volumes of air mixed will produce a 'Rolling Fire' which is termed a diffuse explosion. This will push out walls, singe human hair and eyebrows, and set clothing alight. There will be no hard detonation; rather a whoosh and the whole place will be on fire.'

We know that at the Crystal Palace no one had their hair or eyebrows singed, and no one had their clothing set alight. Burning clothing, once it commences to flame, causes the wearer to suffer serious burns. No one suffered burns at the Crystal Palace. The only injuries were sustained by firemen, and these of a minor nature – cuts from broken class and splintered woodwork such as Mr. Stone experienced. Had a diffuse explosion taken place, then Mr. Sydney Clark and Mr. Frank Tullett would have been seriously burned. So also would Mr. Legg, who saw the streak of flame running across the Egyptian Court like a will-o-the-wisp. It was this phenomenon which gave Sir Henry Buckland his cue to seize hold of gas, and attempt to make it the culprit. Sir Henry was undoubtedly among the foremost rank of showmen and entrepreneurs, but he certainly was not either a chemist or a physicist; a basic grounding in one or other would have told him that gas was a non-starter, sure to fall apart under scrutiny.

In order to verify the accuracy of Kirk's findings, I was able to arrange for a small experiment to be set up. This consisted of a pressure vessel with armoured glass observation windows, standard equipment for fire tests involving a range of gases. The pressure vessel contained timber, furniture-covering materials and samples of textiles used in clothing. The pressure vessel was charged with Kirk's ratio – one of town gas to ten of air – and ignited by an electric arc. The effect can best be described as being like the flame of a blow-lamp quickly turned on and off leaving the timber, furniture-covering and textiles burning furiously. The pressure value obtained within the vessel, recorded on a gauge, was about 80lb sq in, sufficient to push out walls and partitions of average building values. Here, indeed, was Kirk's Law vividly demonstrated, leaving no doubt as to the horrific fate which would have overtaken Mr. Clark, Mr. Tullett and Mr. Legg, had a diffuse gas explosion occurred at Crystal Palace.

The sequence of events within the pressure vessel was recorded on cine film, and played back at slow motion. The blow-lamp flame described above could be clearly seen to roll upwards to the top of the pressure vessel (the ceiling of a room) and, not unlike waves rolling on to a beach, the blow lamp flame was seen to consist of a rapid series of flames rolling on top of each other – Kirk's 'rolling fire.'

Inflammable liquids

In order to establish if Mr. Legg's transient coloured flames racing like a will-o-the-wisp along the floor had any scientific basis in fact, I turned to H. M. Fire Research Station Borehamwood, Hertfordshire, the foremost organisation of its type in the world. Mr. P. M. P. Smart, acting for the Director of Fire Research told me in a letter that '…Whisky has too high a flash point and petrol does not fit the colour description, but chemicals such as acetone, cellulose nitrate and methylated spirit are all possibilities.' This indicates the presence of one or the other of those inflammable liquids having a flash point below room temperature, but that town gas could be discounted, because it is much lighter than air and unlikely to stay at floor level. A serious gas leak would more likely have resulted in an explosion soon after the fire started.

In order to confirm Mr. Smart's findings I arranged for a further experiment, using flat smooth surfaces as representing floors. Three tests, with each of the liquids indicated by Mr. Smart as being worthy of consideration, were carried out. Ignition was by open flame, and with each liquid the results were similar; bluish-green flames racing and flickering across the surfaces. Having watched these experiments I knew that I was seeing Mr. Legg's stream of flame racing along the floor like a will-o-the-wisp.

Mr. Smart did, however, suggest one possible alternative 'A fairly fresh application on the smooth floor asphalt of lacquer or polish containing volatile solvents could produce a similar effect in the presence of an igniting source.' I was only able to reproduce this with domestic floor polish when the surfaces were considerably heated.

Moreover, floor polish was not used at the Crystal Palace as a rule, because of the danger to the public of slipping and suffering injury, which would have left Sir Henry Buckland open to claims for compensation or damages.

They ripped up the floor boards

The fire of Sunday 30th December, 1866 was stopped by a simple expedient. The lone watchman on duty must have been well trained in the art of fire containment. Having made certain that the fire brigades were alerted, he took practical steps toward stopping the fire. He ran outside on to Crystal Palace Parade mobilising what help was to hand among passers-by. Together, they went back into the north nave and, seizing what tools were to hand e.g. hand-axes and crowbars, began ripping up the timber floor at the point of intersection between the north nave and north transept. This resolute action created a fire break, and cut short the supply of fuel upon which the fire was feeding, i.e. the timber floor. This undoubtedly helped retard the spread of fire into the nave.

Gas Board records

25-May-36	(Gas Board letter to Sir Henry Buckland)	I understand that a test was carried out yesterday and with all known points of supply turned off your meters were still passing gas, equivalent to an annual cost of £400.
8-Jun-36 & 9-Jun-36	Reservoir Meter isolated and all known points of supply shut off, including 5in "Exhibition Main"	Losing 13 cubic feet per hour "unaccounted for"
	Egyptian Court Meter Outlet circuit plus the 5in "Exhibition Main" isolated and all known points of supply shut off.	Losing 100 cubic feet per hour "unaccounted for".
	Egyptian Court meter outlet circuit alone isolated and all known points of supply shut off including 5in "Exhibition Main"	Losing 12½ cubic feet per hour "unaccounted for".
Therefore approximately 90 cubic feet per hour is being lost through the 5in Exhibition Main. Every supply to the 5in main was traced and where the pipe was of no use, the main cock was turned off, or if not possible, the pipe line was disconnected by the main and plugged. 25 leaking main cocks were also found.		
14-Jun-36	5in main on the outlet circuit of the Exhibition Court Meter, 50 cubic feet was passing through. 10 cubic feet was being used by the Fireman's Office.	Losing 40 cubic feet per hour "unaccounted for".
16-Jun-36		Losing 40 cubic feet per hour "unaccounted for". c1,000ft of unwanted pipe line shut off from the main.
20-Jun-36	(Gas Board letter to Sir Henry Buckland)	5x2in risers supply hundreds of feet of unwanted pipelines throughout the length of one side of the building. These mainly used to supply gas lamps.
26-Jun-36	(Sir Henry Buckland letter to Gas Board)	Instructions given to staff to remove all disused gas pipes, lamps, brackets, etc. "It is evident however, we shall not even then have eradicated the trouble..."
1-Jul-36	(Gas Board letter to Sir Henry Buckland)	I regret to learn that it has not been possible to reduce to any extent the quantity of gas unaccounted for.
5-Sep-36	1in riser Concert Hall (supplying galleries)	Shut off
	1¼in riser Ambassadors Room	Leak stopped
	1¼in riser Disused lamp bracket	Shut off
	¾in plug Persian Court	Leak stopped
	1in riser Persian Court	Shut off
	½in bend Persian Court (supplying disused lamps in grounds)	Cut off & plugged
	2in pipe Persian Court (supplying grounds)	Cut off & plugged
	½in pipe Fine Art Store	Cut off & plugged
	1in cock Disused supply	Shut off
	½in bend	Cut off & plugged
	½in Monkey House	Cut off & plugged
	1¼in cock Organ Grandstand (supplying disused lights)	Shut off
	½in Lavatories (supplying many old services)	Shut off

Penge Urban District Council
FIRE BRIGADE

Date   Time of call

Chief Officer's Report of Fire, on *30th November 1936 at 7-59 PM*

Discovery and cause

I submit details of the fire which occurred at the Crystal Palace on Monday, 30th November 1936.

(A plan of the area and a selection of photographs will be laid on the table).

A fireman employed by the Crystal Palace Trustees discovered the fire while patrolling the building. He stated that he noticed a smell of smoke when he reached the Egyptian Hall, but, being unable to trace its source, he went back to the adjacent boiler house to attend to the boiler. He returned to the Egyptian Hall between 7.30 and 7.40 p.m. and found that the amount of smoke had increased. In the course of further search he found that the female staff mess room was well alight. He attempted, unsuccessfully, to extinguish the fire with the jet from a hydrant, and another fireman was sent to call the Penge Fire Brigade.

The first call given to the London Fire Brigade was received by fire alarm at 8 p.m. at West Norwood Fire Station and further calls were received by exchange telephone at New Cross Fire Station.

Attendance

At 8.10 p.m. a "District" call message was sent back from the fire followed by a "Brigade" call at 8.15 p.m.

The attendance from the London Fire Brigade was ultimately increased to:

53 pumps and 8 dual-purpose appliances = 61 pumping units.

4 turntable ladders

2 emergency tenders 7 lorries

2 hose lorries 2 tenders

1 canteen van 12 cars

381 officers and men

The attendance from other brigades was as follows:-

Penge Fire Brigade

1 combination

8 men

Croydon Fire Brigade

1 combination

1 pump-ladder

2 cars

11 men

Beckenham Fire Brigade

2 pumps

13 men

Weather conditions

There was a strong northwest wind blowing which veered to west at times.

Control of operations

The County boundary runs through the front part of the Palace but practically all of the buildings are in the Penge area. The London Fire Brigade took charge at the request of the Chief of the Penge Fire Brigade.

Description of the buildings

The Crystal Palace, which was erected on the crest of Anerley Hill about 1854, consisted of a large main building about 1,400 ft. x 450 ft., with a large Central Transept and a smaller Southern Transept. It was constructed of a cast-iron frame-work, on which was hung wooden framing for the glass, roof and sides. In height the building varied from 60 to 160 ft. A number of galleries on each side extended the length of the building. These had wooden flooring and were supported by cast-iron stanchions. Access to them was provided by a number of broad wooden staircases. There were towers about 250 feet in height at each end of the building. That at the southern end adjoined the main building but that at the northern was separated from the main building by an ornamental lake. Another building which adjoined the main building on the south side and
extended for about 1,000 ft. along Anerley Hill was, together with part of the South Tower, occupied by Baird Television, Ltd.

Altogether the building covered an area of about twenty-eight acres.

Account of the fire

On the arrival of the first London Fire Brigade appliances the Central Transept was well alight and within a few minutes the greater part of it had collapsed.

The earlier appliances experienced great difficulty in getting to the fire owing to the large crowds of people which gathered to watch the fire.

With no dividing walls to resist its advance and fanned by the strong northwest wind the fire spread rapidly. The shape of the building also assisted the spread of the fire. It quickly involved the South Transept, and threatened to involve the South Tower and the building occupied by the Baird Television Co. In view of the serious consequences which would have been involved had this Tower collapsed, the major efforts of the Brigade were directed to preventing the fire from spreading at this point. In this the Brigade were successful although the fire involved part of the Television building and reached to within 15 ft. of the Tower. As additional appliances arrived many branches were got to work on this side of the fire. Difficulties were still being experienced owing to the approaches to the Crystal Palace being filled with the motor vehicles of sightseers, and Scotland Yard was informed of the traffic congestion. Some crews had to leave their appliances at some distance from the fire and make their way on foot through the crowds to obtain their instructions. The arrival of the mobile Police, however, improved matters in this respect. With more pumps getting to work the water supply was proving inadequate and collector pumping was resorted to. A number of pumps drew water from the ornamental lake by the North Tower and augmented the supply of those at work along Crystal Palace Parade.

With the wind veering west the fire began to spread in the direction of the North Tower and, in spite of additional jets being played on this side, within a short time little more than the iron structure of the northern section of the building remained.

Matters gradually improved, and at 11.45 p.m. it was possible to send back the "stop" message.

The Duty was left and turned over to the Penge Fire Brigade at 5.0 p.m. on Tuesday 1st December

Damage

A range of buildings of one, two and three floors and basement covering an area of about 1,400x1,000ft., used as showrooms, studios, workshops, offices and store; about two-thirds of buildings and contents burned and fallen down; rest of buildings and South Tower and contents damaged by fire, heat, smoke and water.

Cause

It has not been possible so far to ascertain the cause of this fire.

Injuries

One sub-officer and three firemen were slightly injured. They sustained burns from molten lead which dropped from the roof.

New hose lorry

The specially designed hose lorry, which was recently placed in commission, attended the fire and proved of considerable value in conveying hose quickly to the various points at which it was required.

Other appliances available

At the height of the fire the following appliances were available in the Brigade for dealing with other fires:-

12 escapes

39 dual-purpose appliances and 2 pumps = 41 pumping units

7 turntable ladders

Staff Section Z

Staff Section Z was in attendance and performed useful work in relieving the officers who were fighting the fire from responsibility for the supplies of food, petrol and oil and for the arrangements for relief.

The visit of the Duke of Kent

His Royal Highness The Duke of Kent attended the fire and was shown round by your Chairman and the Chief Officer of the Brigade.

Broadcasts

The B.B.C. broadcast a short eye-witness account of this fire following the late news summary on Monday, 30th November, 1936, and on Tuesday, 1st December, 1936, the Divisional Officer, Major F. W. Jackson, D.S.O. gave a short talk in 'In Town Tonight' and in the 10 o'clock news bulletin on the work of the Brigade at the fire.

Building control

The premises do not come under the Council's building control either from the Building Act point of view or as regards public entertainment.

These premises held music and dancing and stage plays licences from the Council for a number of years until 1900, after which time the building ceased to come under the Council's jurisdiction. The buildings have for many years been regarded as far below the standard required by the Council for places of public entertainment.

In 1911, in connection with the Festival of Empire, the Home Office asked the Chief Officer to report on the building. It was stated that the fire extinguishing equipment was inadequate and it was also suggested that the Palace authorities should consult an outside architect for general advice. This was not done.

In 1932, orchestral concerts for school children began to be held, and the question arose as to whether the standard of safety was such as to enable the Council to agree to the attendance of London children at such concerts. Certain improvements were suggested by the Council on the recommendations of the Architect and Chief Officer as a condition of its participation in these concerts, but only a few of such recommendations were carried out. The Architect advised in 1934, however, that the building was not suitable for children's performances and they were discontinued. The Council does not appear have been concerned in the building since that time.

RECOMMENDATION

That a copy of this report be passed to the Entertainments Committee as a matter of interest.

CJW

Chief Officer, L.F.B. 4/12/36

How called	*Crystal Palace Fireman by GPO. T. Syd. 6715*
Time of Leaving	*8.0pm MOTOR COMBINATION*
Place	*Crystal Palace. Crystal Palace Parade Upper Norwood SE*
Description of Premises	*Crystal Palace*
Tenant of Premises	*Crystal Palace Trustees* *Such Tenants. Mecca Cafes Ltd. Baird Television*
Owner of Premises	Crystal Palace Trustees
Appliances and Men present	*PENGE. Motor Combination 7 men & Supt.* *2 Motor pumps, 1 Motor Tender, 11 men & Chief Officer* *CROYDON 2 Motor Appliances, 2 Cars, 8 men & Chief Officer* *LONDON 8 Dual Purpose Machines, 53 Pumps, 4 Turntable Ladders* *12 Cars, 2 Fire Lorries. 7 Lorries & 2 Emergency Tenders* *1 Canteen Van, 381 officers & men, Salvage Corps* *3 Motor Tenders, 1 Motor Car, 22 men & Chief officers.*
How extinguished,	Motor Pumps & hydrants. & Motor Pumps working from Lake. Number of lines of Hose used, etc.
Cause of Fire	Unknown
General Remarks as to Damage, etc.	*A range of buildings of one, two and three floors and basements covering an area of about 1,400ft x 1,000ft used as Showrooms, Studios, Workshop, Offices & Stores, about two thirds of buildings & contents burned & fallen down, rest of Buildings & South Tower & contents damaged by Fire, Heat, Smoke & Water. Gates broken open Tunnel approach slightly by Fire, Heat, Smoke & Water.*

Particulars of Insurance from London Salvage Corps

Building

Gardner Mountain & D'Ambrumenil Ltd
Insurance Brokers. 3 Old St. E.C.2 Telephone No. London Wall 4251
Building £110,000
Organ £10,000

Mecca Cafes

Alliance Insurance Co. Ltd. Bartholomew Lane E.C.2 Telephone No. London Wall 2345
Contents £14,350
Consequential Loss £3,500

Baird Television

Northern Assurance Co Ltd. Moorgate E.C.2 Telephone No. MET 1262
Amount £73,000

Badminton Club

Atlas Insurance Co Ltd 92 Cheapside. E.C.2 Telephone No. NAT 7600
Amount £650   *Grateful thanks to Kent Fire Brigade Museum*

METROPOLITAN POLICE REPORTS
Croydon Station "Z" division

1st December 1936

Outbreak of Fire

A.2

At 7.40.p.m. on 30th November 1936 a very serious fire occurred at The Crystal Palace, Sydenham, owned by the Crystal Palace Trustees, General Manager Sir Henry Buckland who resides within the grounds of the Palace.

It was discovered by Mr. William Charles Ferguson, No. 28, Kingswood Road, Penge, Crystal Palace Staff Foreman, who has stated: "The first I saw was that the ladies' rest room, at the rear of the General Offices, was ablaze; that would be about twenty minutes to eight. At that time, the north end of the rest room was well alight. With Staff Foreman Clark I got a hose to bear on it. Realising it was too big for us I got on to the telephone exchange at about 7.50.p.m. and asked the girl to call the Fire Brigade. Then Clark and I continued to play water on the fire until forced to leave by the galleries falling; I have no idea what caused it."

The first Police Officer to arrive was P.C. 155 "Z" Parkin[1], who arrived at 7.54.p.m. and called the Penge Fire Brigade at 7.55.p.m. Inspector Hussey "Z" Divn. and P.C. 419 "Z" Woolhead, attended at 7.57.p.m.

The first brigade to arrive was The Penge Fire Brigade at 8.03.p.m. followed by that of Beckenham at 8.05.p.m. Following these at short intervals were 61 Pumping Units, 4 Turntable Ladders, and various Mobile Units of the L.C.C. Fire Brigade, with a total of 350 Firemen, all under the control of Major Morris.

The cause of the fire is unknown.

INJURY

There was one case of personal injury and that was to Fireman E. Freeborn, age 37, of 40a Quinton Street, Earlsfield, who was treated at Norwood Cottage Hospital at 10.30.pm, by Doctor Starbrook for burns to the face. But after treatment was allowed to go.

Many cases of fainting by women occurred in the crowds and these were dealt with by local members of the St. John's Ambulance Brigade.

DAMAGE

Crystal Palace

With the exception of the North and South Towers, the general main building was completely destroyed. The value cannot at present be estimated but it must be considerable. Premises insured.

Baird Television Company, 66, Haymarket, W.

This company are sub-tenants, and occupy a portion of the south wing as laboratories, and this was wholly destroyed. Value cannot be estimated.

Other Buildings

These buildings within the curtilage of the Palace but not attached to the main building were not involved in the conflagration.

1 Altered by hand to Parker

Motor cars

Private Car, BBY 351[2], owner at present unknown, which was left locked in the main entrance was in danger of becoming involved in the fire and the window was broken by P.C. 155 "Z" Parker in order to release the brake and push it to safety.

The P.C.'s truncheon was damaged in this action (scratched) and this will be dealt with separately.

Five other cars were removed from the main entrance to safety without damage.

Houses in vicinity

"The Knole"[3], 4, Crystal Palace Parade, Upper Norwood, owned by Lady Elizabeth Hamilton, 132, College Road, Upper Norwood, occupied by Mrs. Cynthia Marks – 100 yards of Oak Pale Fencing broken down by presence of enormous crowds assembled. Owner and occupier informed.

No.1, Sydenham Hill, Unoccupied, owned by Messrs Berkeley and Berkeley, 22 Upper Grosvenor St., W.1. – Twenty feet of wooden pale fencing broken down by pressure from the crowd.

No. 18, Palace Parade "Palace Furnishers" Upper Norwood, owned and occupied by Mr. Brian – four feet of iron guttering at the rear of the premises broken by persons climbing to the roof. Owner informed.

No. 4, Farquhar Road, Upper Norwood, owned by Dulwich College Estate Offices, Dulwich Village, S.E.26 – Twenty-Five yards of wooden fencing broken down by crowd pressure. Owners informed.

A very serious danger was narrowly averted by the Fire Brigade preventing the fire reaching the South Tower. The tower abuts Anerley Hill and had it fallen the consequences would have been disastrous to those houses in the vicinity. Police were held in readiness to warn all residents at the first sign of danger.

This fire spread very rapidly and within half an hour the whole building seemed involved.

Immediately crowds were attracted and great difficulty was experienced in dealing with them. Aid from adjoining divisions was applied for and found very necessary. Whilst it is impossible to estimate it is generally agreed that no less than 100,000 people assembled in the vicinity of the Palace.

Vehicular traffic was also enormous. An early diversion had been made but outside that diversion congestion existed for some time by sightseers, motorists, etc., until police were able to restore more or less normal working.

Whilst I have had not a complaint I feel that some of the late arrivals of the fire brigade must have experienced some difficulty in getting through, although every effort is generally made by the public to facilitate the Fire Brigade.

At 8.10.p.m. it became necessary to send to surrounding stations for "Aid". These commenced to arrive at 8.25.p.m. and continued up to 11.30.p.m., when a total of 2

---

2 Known to be a green Riley first registered January 1936

3 The correct spelling the house name is "The Knoll"

Superintendents (Superintendent White "P" and myself), 2 Chief Inspectors, 7 Senior Divisional Inspectors, 21 Inspectors, 62 Sergeants, and 551 Constables, and 5 P.C.s Mounted, were in attendance, all of whom were required.

At 11.10.p.m. a message was sent to the Commissioner's office, stating that no more Aid was required. Dismissal commenced at 12 Mdt, and the final dismissal, other than those remaining all night, was at 3.25.a.m. Even at 3.15.a.m. probably 500 people were still there.

Just before 12 Mdt the Duke of Kent arrived and remained till about 3.a.m.

D.A.C.[4] and C.C.4[5] Area were present nearly the whole of the time.

Arising from this fire are two point of interest:

    1. The Special Constabulary attached to Gipsy Hill Police Station turned out practically to a man and I am sending a letter of thanks to their Commandant.

    2. Rotarians – Three members of this body voluntarily attended Wallington Station with cars to convey Police wherever required.

They are – Mr F. Sutton-Smith, "Esh Shem", 1 The Mead, Wallington.

                Mr. S.J. Hollands, "Clematis", 83 Plough Lane, Wallington.

                Mr. H.O. Keith, 6 Foxley Hill Road, Purley.

I shall be sending a letter to each expressing our appreciation and thanks.

Superintendent "Z"

Copies forwarded to
S.3., Receiver,
and D.A.C.4.

---

4 Deputy Assistant Commissioner

5 Chief Constable Area 4

METROPOLITAN POLICE-TELEGRAM

1st December 1936
To: Officer i/c Transport

From: S.D. Insp. J. Pollock at Croydon
Forwarded at: 3.a.m.

Re fire at Crystal Palace, 2 Insps. 3 P.S.s. and 32 P.C.s were conveyed from Croydon at 10.p.m., 30.11.36 by L.P.T.B. bus ordered from South Croydon Garage to College Road Crystal Palace. Bus dismissed at 12 midnight on arrival. L.P.T.B. informed by telephone at 2.30.a.m. 1st December, 1936.

J. Pollock - S.D. Inspector
D.1 Transport - Lambeth Garage
1st December 1936

FIRE AT CRYSTAL PALACE 30/11/36

The undermentioned Tender Drivers and Civilian Drivers were engaged on Duty in connection with the above

DRIVER	TIME DESPATCHED	TIME RETURNED	VEHICLE
Mr. Bates	10.p.m.	1.a.m.	-----
Dr. Buxton	10.p.m.	12.30.a.m.	213.G
Dr. Jones	9.30.p.m.	12.30.a.m.	220.G
Dr. Hiles	11.p.m.	12.00 midnight	-----
P.C. Drewett	8.30.p.m.	3.22.a.m.	222.G
P.C. Glanfield	10.30.p.m.	?	208.G
P.C. French	11.50.p.m.	3.43.a.m.	209.G
P.C. Rea	11.50.p.m.	3.18.a.m.	225.G
P.C. Richardson	11.50.p.m.	7.00.a.m.	219.G
P.C. Bedford	11.00.p.m.	7.17.a.m.	221.G
P.C. Franklin	11.30.p.m.	7.10.a.m.	562.A
P.C. Taylor	11.50.p.m.	5.53.a.m.	215.G
P.C. Blandford	12.15.a.m.	6.53.a.m.	213.G
P.C. Asquith	11.50.p.m.	3.22.a.m.	211.G
P.C. Worby 'G'	12.15.a.m.		220.G
P.C. Venner'G'	12.15.a.m.		226.G
P.C. Perkins 'G'	12.15.a.m.		223.G
P.C. Wooley 'G'	12.15.a.m.		224.G
P,C. Evans 'H'	12.15.a.m.		212.G

o/c Transport
In addition to the above mentioned vehicles, one L.P.T.B. 56 seater bus was requisitioned at 10p.m. & dismissed at 12 midnight for 37 officers of Z Divn.

J. Pollock

National Archives file MEPO 2/4350

From: **In the wake of disaster – 200 years of The Toplis and Harding Group,** **by David Wainwright. Published by Quiller Press Ltd, 1990. ISBN 1 870948 29 7**

In December 1936, Graham Harding dealt with the Crystal Palace insurance claim.

The managing-director of the Crystal Palace company (which managed the building on behalf of trustees), Sir Henry Buckland, said that while it had cost £1,350,000 to build, its replacement cost would be between £4 million and £5 million. It was insured for £110,000, and the organ was separately insured for £10,000. Insurances on the contents – mainly catering and exhibition equipment – totalled a further £70,000. The low figure was based on the fact that when the building had been bought from the South Kensington Great Exhibition organizers for the nation, in 1911, the price paid was £200,000 (and most of that was attributable to the cost of the Sydenham site).

On the instructions of the leading insurers Cuthbert Heath of Lloyd's, Graham Harding was one of the first on the scene on the day after the fire, acting on behalf of Lloyd's. His report was one of the shortest he ever wrote: it was on a half-sheet of paper. There was no question but that the Crystal Palace was a total loss: nothing was recoverable. Harding recommended that the claim should be paid in full. Exactly one week after the fire the Crystal Palace trustees received a cheque from Lloyd's underwriters for £120,000, being £110,000 for the insurances effected on the structure, and £10,000 for the insurances for the organ. It can scarcely have given the trustees any joy.

It was not, however, strictly true that nothing survived. In the midst of the Crystal Palace there had been an aquarium, filled with goldfish. For a day or two after the fire, they had been written off as 'missing, believed boiled'. Then they were found, still swimming around, though discoloured.

Entry in the underwriters' book of C. E. Heath, showing that the claim of the Trustees of the Crystal Palace was settled four days after the fire

Requests for a Public Enquiry and the
Parliamentary Question re BBC broadcast

67 Anerley Park
Anerley, S.E.
1st December 1936

Dear Sir

I feel that it is someone's duty amongst your constituents to call your attention to the disastrous loss the district has suffered & far more than a local calamity... a national loss in the total destruction of the Crystal Palace last night – surely some immediate public enquiry should be instituted into the matter – as to the origin of the fire, and also what means were in existence to have avoided such a catastrophe.

When one reads in the morning papers that the manager stated "my two firemen were trying to extinguish the flames"! – surely such a monster building as the Crystal Palace should have had at least an adequate staff of firemen on night duty – for such a building as the C.P. 1850 of floor space in length! Surely two men in charge became preposterous. Surely this seems gross mis management if not criminal neglect.

Perhaps you will call attention to the matter in the proper quarter at your early opportunity.

Yours very faithfully
Walter J. May

Major Sir E. J. Campbell
H. of C.

RESPONSE

I have ascertained that the Home Secretary has no power to hold an enquiry into the Crystal Palace fire, about which you have sent me one or two letters from constituents. There is no power, except in the City of London under a special Act, to hold a "fire inquest" in cases where no fatalities have occurred.

Sir Edward Campbell, M.P.
House of Commons,
S.W.1

Chambers & Co. (Dyers Ltd)

Head Office:
15 Oakfield Road
Penge, S.E.20
5th December 1936

Telegrams:
CHAMBERS DYERS PENGE
Telephone SYDENHAM 7078-9

The Home Secretary
Whitehall, S.W.1

Sir, As a resident close to the Crystal Palace and as one who has for sometime taken an active interest in its welfare ask you to have an investigation made into the circumstances of its disastrous destruction. I have two men in my employ who inform me they knew the Palace was on fire at 7.40 p.m. on the 30th. November and were able to get to the Palace Parade by 7.50 p.m. when the fire was well away, yet the Penge Fire Brigade did not receive the call until 7.59 p.m. I think in justice to all a very full enquiry should be made by competent Officials and any praise or blame attached to those upon whose shoulders it should fall, as from the information I have received it would seem had the Fire Brigade been called the fire could have been arrested and the Palace saved or a large portion.

In view of the insured value and the value as announced by Sir Henry Buckland it would suggest that possibly other Public Buildings may not be insured to the extent they should be and same should be re-valued by independent professional valuers to bring sane up to the standard conditions of today.

I am, Sir,
Yours obediently,
Russell S. Barnett

12th December 1936

RESPONSE

Sir,

I am directed by the Secretary of State to refer to your letter of the 5th instant, in which it is suggested that an investigation should be made into the circumstances of the fire which occurred recently at the Crystal Palace, and to say that he has no power to make such an enquiry.

I am,
Sir,
Your obedient Servant,

R. S. Barnett, Esq.
C/o Messrs. Chambers & Company (Dyers) Limited
15 Oakfield Road
Penge, S.E.20

House of Commons Parliamentary Question
Daily Debates
Oral Answers – 8/12/1936
BROADCASTING (NEWS ANNOUNCEMENTS).

63. Mr. ANSTRUTHER-GRAY asked the Postmaster-General whether he will request the British Broadcasting Corporation to discontinue their present policy of including in the news programme announcements of fires or disturbances at present taking place in London, as being liable to cause serious interference with fire brigade and ambulance services?

The ASSISTANT POSTMASTER-GENERAL (Sir Walter Womersley): I will convoy my hon. Friend's suggestion to the British Broadcasting Corporation.

Mr. ANSTRUTHER-GRAY: Is my hon. Friend aware that, during the recent fire at the Crystal Palace, when the news was broadcast, thousands of people flocked to the spot by motor car and otherwise, and caused serious interference, and will he bring that point to the attention of the British Broadcasting Corporation?

Sir W. WOMERSLEY: I am aware that crowds did flock to the fire, but I am also aware that, in the broadcast issued by the British Broadcasting Corporation, the following statement was made:

"Fire engines are still making all speed to the spot and we suggest that, in view of the difficulties confronting the police, people should not go to the fire and so make matters worse for them. In any case, cars cannot get near the scene."

Mr. ANSTRUTHER-GRAY: Is not the best way to prevent people going to the fire not to tell them that it is burning?

Sir W. WOMERSLEY: My hon. Friend must realise that this fire could be seen for a few miles.

The Commissioner has no record that this question has ever been raised before, and no previous complaints of this nature have been received from either the Fire Brigade or the Ambulance Service.

On this occasion, however, there is little doubt that the broadcast made by the B.B.C. at 9-3 p.m. [sic] did attract a considerable number of extra people and cars to the scene of the fire, thereby increasing the embarrassment of the police and the Fire Brigade.

For Commissioner of the Police of the Metropolis 8.12.1936
National Archives file HO187/1814

**The full transcript of the broadcast can be read in
The Crystal Palace Foundation book "The Crystal Palace is on Fire!"**

London County Council
Report of the Fire Brigade and Main Drainage Committee.

10th December, 1936

Crystal Palace fire.

1. – We report details of the fire which occurred at the Crystal Palace on Monday, 30th November 1936. A plan of the buildings and photographs of the fire will be exhibited in the ambulatory of the Council chamber.

The Crystal Palace consisted of a large main building about 1,400 feet by 450 feet, with a large central transept and a smaller southern transept. It was constructed of a cast-iron framework, on which was hung wooden framing for the glass roof and sides. In height the building varied from 60 to 160 feet. A number of galleries on each side extended the length of the building. These had wooden flooring and were supported by cast-iron stanchions. Access to them was provided by a number of broad staircases. Towers about 250 feet in height had been built at each end of the building. That at the southern end adjoined the main building but that at the northern was separated from the main building by an ornamental lake. Another building, which adjoined the main building on the south which extended for about 1,000 feet along Anerley-hill, was occupied by Baird Television, Limited, occupied part of the south tower. Altogether the buildings covered an area of about 28 acres.

A fireman employed by the Crystal Palace Trustees discovered the fire while patrolling the building on the evening of 30th November, 1936. The first call given to the London fire brigade was received by fire alarm at 8 p.m. at West Norwood fire station and further calls were received by exchange telephone at New Cross fire station. At 8.10 p.m. a "district" call message was sent back from the fire by a "brigade" call at 8.15 p.m. The attendance from the London fire brigade was ultimately increased to 53 pumps; 8 dual-purpose appliances; 4 turntable ladders; 2 emergency tenders; 7 lorries; 2 tenders; 1 canteen van; 12 cars; 381 officers and men. Most appliances experienced considerable difficulty in reaching the fire owing to the crowds of spectators.

The county boundary runs through the front part of the Palace but practically the whole of the buildings are in Penge. The chief officer of the London fire brigade took charge at the request of the chief officer of the Penge brigade. In addition to the Penge brigade, the Croydon and Beckenham fire brigades also attended.

On the arrival of the first London fire brigade appliances the central transept was well alight and within a few minutes the greater part of it had collapsed. With no dividing walls to resist its advance and fanned by a strong north-west wind, the fire spread rapidly. The shape of the building also assisted the spread of the fire, which quickly involved the south transept and threatened to involve the south tower and the adjoining building occupied by Baird Television, Limited. In view of the serious consequences which would have been involved had this tower collapsed, the main efforts of the brigade were directed to preventing the fire from spreading to it. The efforts were successful, although the fire involved part of the adjoining building and was only checked within 15 feet of the tower.

With additional appliances in action the water supply was proving inadequate and "collective" pumping had to be resorted to. A number of pumps drew water from the ornamental lake by the north tower and augmented the supply of those at work along Crystal Palace-parade.

With the wind veering west, the fire began to spread in the direction of the north tower also and in spite of additional jets being played on this side, within a short time little more than the iron structure of the northern section of the building remained. The north tower itself, which is detached from the main building, was preserved intact.

Before midnight the fire was under control. The duty was left and turned over to the brigade at 5 p.m. on Tuesday, 1st December, 1936.

It has not been possible so far to ascertain the cause of the fire.

EDWARD CRUSE, CHAIRMAN

Resolved – That the report be received.

FIRE AT THE CRYSTAL PALACE

Report by the Department of Scientific and Industrial Research
Building Research Station, Garston, Watford, Hertfordshire

An inspection of the results of the fire at the Crystal Palace revealed the following points of interest –

1. Confirmation of the extreme vulnerability of unprotected structural steel. As far as could be seen failure took place generally by the breaking of the cast iron supporting columns as a result of the bending stresses induced in them by the deflection of the girders. No signs ware observed of failure at cleat connections.

2. The reinforced concrete staircases on the south side of the building were comparatively little damaged, although the transformation of the gravel aggregate to a pink and white colour and the presence of molten glass suggested that considerable temperatures had been attained in the vicinity. Damage was confined to surface spalling about ⅛ in. deep.

3. Under the west staircase a buffet had been ignited and completely gutted. The same evidence of temperature was apparent, and the circumstances suggest that a fairly fierce, though possibly brief, fire raged under the floor slab forming the middle landing of the staircase which was about 15 feet above ground level. The underside of this slab was pitted over the major part of its surface to a depth of ⅛ in. to ¼ in., but no reinforcement had been exposed.

4. A reinforced concrete column in the centre of the buffet was severely spalled at the corners, the reinforcement being partly exposed to view.

The inspection was carried out by Messrs. Cowley and Davies on the 23rd December, 1936

National Archives file Department of Scientific & Industrial Research DSIR4/2728

The Crystal Palace Fire

NOVEMBER 30th, 1936, 8.0 p.m. I was just finishing dinner, after rather a heavy day, when the telephone rang.

"District call, sir, for the Crystal Palace."

"All right, tell my car to stand by."

From the balcony at the back of my flat on the fourth floor at the new headquarters, I could see the Palace quite clearly in the day-time, and, on stepping outside hurriedly to try to see if there was any sign of a fire, I saw a dull red glow lighting up the whole of the centre transept. Definitely a late call – the fire must have been going at least half an hour before we received our first call – we shall probably lose the whole building! These thoughts flashed through my mind as I hurriedly picked up the phone again.

"Anything further back from the fire yet?"

"No, sir."

"Order my car and tell the Senior Superintendent to mobilize heavily on the surrounding stations. You'll probably have a Brigade call back in a few minutes."

In a minute I was on my way, and as my car left the appliance room, the" duty man" shouted after us: "Brigade call, sir."

Well, that was that. Good-bye to the Crystal Palace in all probability. As I rushed through the streets on my way, I tried to size up the situation as I should probably find it on my arrival. I knew the water-supply was very poor in the vicinity – anyhow, there was the ornamental lake with its open water.

The difficulty here was that the Palace was not our responsibility, practically the whole building was outside the L.F.B. area. We had not inspected it and were not responsible for the inside fire arrangements. Anyhow, no doubt the officers would as usual have the whole situation sized up on my arrival and plenty of branches at work from the lake. There was a very good road running round the Palace, and they could relay the hose along this from our new hose lorry, which was receiving its baptism here.

As my thoughts travelled along these lines, I gradually became conscious that there was something very unusual going on in the streets. I had only just passed Camberwell Green, several miles from the fire, when I noticed that a stream of traffic had already started to move towards the fire-cars, motor cycles, bicycles, boys running, men and women walking hurriedly along, all drawn towards that menacing glow in the sky which by now had appeared over the Palace and was commencing to light up the whole district. Anyhow, damnation to them, getting in my way!

But supposing the same stream has started in other streets. Why not? Probably all streets leading to the Palace were in the same condition. What a ghastly traffic mess when we get there! On went the stream of traffic getting more and more congested the nearer we approached. Within a quarter of a mile of the fire the cars were already parked on each side of the road, and as we reached the top of the hill we were met by an almost solid block of cars. What absolute crass stupidity, private motorists gradually filling up the roads, and here we were faced with about fifty appliances speeding on their way, only to meet a most appalling traffic block before they could get to grips.

After about five minutes of hard work and, I'm afraid, of much harder swearing, we forced our way through the cars, only to find a huge, uncontrolled crowd in the way of the firemen who were trying to get their engines to work. After about five minutes' delay, I managed to find the Superintendent, arranged for a total attendance of sixty-three pumps, and then forced my way through the crowd towards the South Tower, which was still intact.

Fanned by a strong north-west wind, the fire had already spread through the south transept, and it was useless to attempt to do anything here except to save at all cost this tower, 250 feet high. If this caught alight it was almost bound to collapse, probably killing several firemen and some of the crowd in its fall.

Some temporary buildings of wood construction connected the main building with the Tower, and with the wind where it was, it would not take long for this unchecked fire to reach the Tower.

It must have taken me five minutes to reach it, only to find on my arrival a very harassed Principal Officer in charge, with two branches laid on and no water! The hydrants in the vicinity had run bone dry owing to the large amount of water being used on the main building. At that moment the Deputy Chief Officer came up and we had a hurried consultation as to what was to be done. How far had they gone down the road for water? A quarter of a mile. Well, go farther and try series working!

Meanwhile, we sent off messengers to knock off all branches working in front of the main building, where they were doing very little good on account of the huge size of the fire, to try and get some water into the main near the Tower. Still no water, and the fire had by now got well hold of the wooden buildings and was travelling towards the Tower. We got into the nearest available car to see if we could arrange for the new hose lorry to layout a line of hose from the lake round the front of the Palace to the Tower. One good jet would save it. "Impossible, sir. The crowds are too great, and you'll never get it through. In any case, she'll stick in the mud if we move her."

The lorry was standing on a small road by the lake, which had by now become a quagmire owing to the water which was flowing from about fifteen pump radiators, this being the normal method of keeping the engine cool when pumping water on to the fire.

"Well, chance it, she may get through, and we simply must try and get a line of hose to the Tower."

After much wheel spin and skidding, the lorry started off on its long hose-laying trek, through crowds, over hose, a painfully slow business. Meanwhile, we tore back in the car as fast as the crowds and hose would allow, to find the fire actually within a few feet of the Tower, but also to my great relief enough water coming through two branches to stop it. A very near thing. The message to knock off the other branch had done the trick and some water had reached the water main near the Tower.

On reaching the front of the fire again, we found that the wind had veered round to the west and that the fire was spreading into the north transept. By now we had an increased water-supply owing to branches from several pumps working from the lake having been brought up the front of the fire. The Divisional Officer was in charge here, and we decided to risk placing two branches and crews inside the main building to try and stop the fire from travelling along towards the end of this transept.

It was a risk; a large collapse might take place at any moment and a back draught of flame might occur.

The whole transept was heating up rapidly, and unless we could get some water on at once, it would be alight from end to end.

Two crews quickly got to work and stopped the fire from spreading on the ground floor, and it looked as though we had checked it, when in a flash, a huge sheet of flame travelled along the under roof over their heads out of reach of the jets. It was no good then waiting until the roof started to fall and injure these crews, so we had to get them out with their branches as quickly as possible. Within a few minutes, this transept was doomed, no water could possibly check this enormous fire, and we were not going to risk any of the men's lives in what was a hopeless task by placing them farther north in this transept. The only thing left for us to do was to concentrate all the water available at the end of the north transept from the outside to see if we could save anything.

I now had an opportunity to have a really good look at the fire. When officers are at a serious fire that is tending to spread, they simply have no time to see the fire as a whole. The onlookers see it, but a Principal Officer has a very definite job to do, requiring all his energy and concentration. He seldom has time to realize what a magnificent spectacle is taking place until his work is finished, and by then the fire has usually eased down. The building was by now one huge uncontrolled fire from end to end. A huge mass of fire in a building measuring 1400 feet by 450 feet, large enough to have contained the buildings in a large street in the city – a perfectly grand and awe-inspiring spectacle, a fire which, had it occurred in a congested area, no fire brigade could possibly have stopped from spreading to surrounding property and starting another conflagration.

By now, however, our anxieties were at an end. There were no surrounding risks, the South Tower was saved. Shortly after, with a loud roar, the whole of the centre transept collapsed, and it was here that the London Fire Brigade cameraman (we have our own film service) took some really splendid films. He knew just how far in he could stand without getting hurt when the crash came. This film was shown practically all over the world and gave a really splendid picture of the whole fire.

At this period of the fire the total appliances in attendance from London were as follows: 53 pumps, 8 dual purpose appliances, 4 turntable ladders, 2 emergency tenders, 7 lorries, 2 hose lorries, 2 tenders, 1 canteen van, 12 cars, 281 officers and men. Various appliances from other brigades were also present.

Shortly after the centre transept had collapsed, and the fire was beginning to die down, a very agitated messenger rushed up to say that the Duke of Kent had arrived at the fire and would like to see the Chief Officer. He had an equerry with him, and after we had had a look at the fire from the front, I asked him if he would like to have a walk round and see the engines at work from the lake, where the branches were continuing their rather hopeless task of trying to save the end of the north transept. He had arrived in full evening dress from an official dinner, so I suggested that we lend him a helmet, top boots, and a mackintosh. He jumped at the idea, but I wanted if possible to take him round by himself, without his equerry; we could then get away from formalities, and it would be much easier to introduce the officers direct to him, as I felt sure he would prefer this. I therefore gave an officer the tip: "One helmet and one pair of boots only. Say, that's all we can find."

The ruse worked and off we went, leaving the equerry standing in evening dress on the dry road, while the Duke trudged along through all the water and mud that always collects round a large fire.

Well, we all had a splendid time with him, and I was able to introduce to him not only the Principal Officers and Superintendent, but what was of great moment to the Brigade, some of the young Station Officers who had been having a very thick time. One thing I regretted his seeing – our largest radial branches at work, each throwing 500 gall. a minute, and looking for all the world like miniature jets against this huge building.

Like the other members of the Royal Family I have met in connexion with my work, he took the keenest interest in all he saw, asked numerous questions that were always to the point, and I really believe he enjoyed his experience. Anyhow, it was a change from after-dinner speeches!

Before the Duke left the fire I suggested a cup of coffee at the canteen van, to which he readily agreed, so we all gathered round and had steaming hot drinks.

An incident occurred during the fire that only came to my notice when I arrived back at headquarters, and to which I took strong exception. The B.B.C. broadcast an announcement that the Crystal Palace was on fire during the early stages, thereby adding to our difficulties with the already huge crowd there. This untimely announcement sent thousands more to the fire from their homes, who otherwise would not have heard of it until the next morning.

When any disaster has taken place in London, those whose duty it is to attend to it, whether it be Police, Fire Brigade, or any other public service, always have difficulty with the crowd, which invariably gets in the way and makes their work more difficult, and it is absolutely essential that no mention is made about it on the wireless until the work there has been completed. The Police came in for some criticism for allowing this huge traffic muddle, but what on earth could they have done in the short time available?

Remember, I was at the car traffic jam within ten minutes of the District call message, and when one realizes that this road was only one of, say, ten others leading to the Palace, well, how could the Police set up an efficient traffic control on the outskirts of London in that very short time?

This fire, right on the top of a hill, was a magnificent spectacle. It could be seen from all over London, and it produced a problem none of us had foreseen. Even if we had foreseen it, what could we have done? If motorists are so stupid and ill advised as to block up whole streets with their cars in the event of any disaster to which they have driven out of idle curiosity, there should be a law authorizing the heaviest penalties for obstruction.

There is a very interesting point in connexion with this fire, and it relates to the London Building Act. One of the objects of this Act is to regulate, not only the size of the building between the party walls, but what is of greater moment from the Fire Department point of view, to restrict the size of cell or room in the building itself.

The maximum cell originally was 250,000 cubic feet, this being afterwards increased to 500,000. No sooner had that concession been allowed than they began a fight for 1,000,000 cubic feet. This we fought for some years. We do not, however, allow these large cells in London unless the building is protected by automatic sprinklers.

Now the Crystal Palace was an outstanding example of the unrestricted area – one huge cell with no fire walls of any kind. Once let a fire get a hold in a large space of that size, and invariably the Fire Brigade will be powerless to stop it.

"How could a building constructed of glass have burnt so fiercely?" some ask.

How many times have we to meet that same old question? Why should I have to take all these precautions when my building is fire-proof? It isn't the building that burns, but what you put in it. Put celluloid in the latest fire resisting building, and you'll not only burn the celluloid, but probably so damage your building as to necessitate its reconstruction. So with the old Crystal Palace. The contents were nothing more or less than a huge highly inflammable bonfire. Organ, theatre, concert hall, numerous side shows, all constructed of timber, and of considerable age and well dried.

The cause of the fire was never ascertained. It was proved, however, that it started near the organ, the worst fire risk in the building. The whole roof actually burnt, giving the impression that the glass itself was alight. This was due to a large amount of timber having been used in its construction, probably to keep the glass in position.

And so in the space of about four hours disappeared one of London's most famous landmarks, regretted by some but not by others, notably the younger generation!

FIRE! by Major C.C.B. Morris

Memories of Jim Barnard a Bishopsgate fireman

Jim Barnard joined the London Fire Brigade in May 1936 and recalled the Crystal Palace Fire in the November of that year as the first major fire he attended. He was serving at No. 36 Bishopsgate at the time. Many years later he gave this description of it.

"In November we received a call to a fire at Crystal Palace, at least thirty miles from where I was stationed near Liverpool Street Station. The call came in at roughly 7.30-8.00pm. One of our men, Fireman Sullivan, had gone to the top of the fire tower in the drill yard and announced that he could see smoke rising above the city in the distance. Just before the call came we received information from Whitechapel, the Superintendent station, that the fire was a large one and that it was likely we would be ordered on shortly. We were warned to take great care to ring the bell on the appliance when proceeding to the fire because many appliances would be converging from side roads onto the main route through South London. We were told to listen at junctions for other appliances travelling towards Crystal Palace. As you can imagine London was sending many appliances and personnel.

Before we had the order to attend my Station Officer said "Barnard, take your gear off the turntable ladder and put it on the pump, and Mayston take your gear off the pump and put it on the turntable ladder." He then turned to me and said "Barnard, if we are ordered on tonight you will see a fire which you will remember for all your life. You will be able to tell your grandchildren of how you went to the fire at Crystal Palace."

How very true that proved to be.

When we got the call, we proceeded from the station in an open fire pump called the Braidwood type, in which the firemen sat along the length of the appliance with their backs to each other and got dressed. On arriving at the fire, which was immense, we could see the Chief Fire Officer and other senior officers with their silver helmets, in a small group in front of the fire. One of the senior officers told us to set our pump in a particular position and to take branches from our pump into the base of the north tower. The north tower had a small restaurant with a serving counter and cash registers. Opposite the entrance doors through which we entered was a large area of framed glass which separated the restaurant from the interior of the building. Most of that glass had now disappeared and the amount of air being drawn into the fire through the doors where we had entered with our hoses was so strong that we were quite fearful of being drawn into the fire by the very force of the wind. We had to exercise great care holding on to the hose while discharging water into the fire.

The Station Officer later brought another man to take over from me and I was told to walk smartly along the front of the building as if I was on an errand. I was told not to stop and watch anything going on around me or I would be questioned and possibly admonished by a senior officer. I thought this rather strange, although I now understand that I was being given an opportunity to see the fire which I had seen little of from the outside. As I went along, I could see the Chief Officer talking to a number of other people some distance away from the building, I made haste to pass them and was not stopped. One of those people was one of the young Princes. I am not certain, but I believe it to have been the Duke of York. He was a "fire buff" and had been given a uniform by the Chief Officer and often attended the bigger fires. I then retraced my steps back to my previous position.

Round about 10.00 am the following day we were told to make up as the fire was now under control and less appliances were required. We made up our hoses and returned back to the Bishopsgate Fire Station. I seem to remember we got back to Bishopsgate Fire Station just after midday and got home sometime later."

Jim served at Whitechapel during the war, throughout the Blitz, and ended his career as Deputy Chief of Essex. He retired in 1967.   *Firemen Remembered*

Weather reports for 30 November 1936 from the London Weather Centre

Weather forecast for the 24 hours commencing 12 noon G.M.T.
30 November 1936. S.E. England.
Moderate west to northwest wind, some light rain early in the period,
becoming fair later; mild.

Weather forecast for 6pm at Croydon 30 November 1936

Barometric pressure – 1013.4 Falling

Wind direction – West North West changeable

Wind speed – Force 5 (19-24 miles per hour)

Temperature – 50°

Humidity – 65%

Visibility – 6 Moderate visibility 6 ½ miles

Cloud form – Low layer of Stratus or Stratus Cumulus

Amount of cloud – Overcast sky with a few small traces of low cloud

Cloud base – 5700 feet

State of ground – Wet

Weather – Slight dust haze

Transcripts of some sections of newspaper articles mentioned in the book
All are dated 1st December 1936

Report by a *Daily Express* Staff Reporter.

Sir Henry Buckland said to me:– 'I left the office at half-past five, and everything was alright then. The only occupants of the Palace were our own fire brigade and a musical society who were practising.

'At 7:15pm I went out to post a letter after dinner and saw a flame behind the offices, which are in the centre of the main building, almost on Crystal Palace Parade. I hurried in and found my firemen already at work.

I then hurried to warn the musicians, and they and their instruments were safely got out.'

Daily Express

'My Life's Work Is Finished' – Sir H. Buckland

'I saw a red glow and raced along to the seat of the fire, shouting for the three firemen who were on duty. The firemen and my daughter responded at once. While the firemen attacked the flames, my daughter ran across to the other side of the Palace where the Palace orchestra was rehearsing. They got the south doors open and escaped that way.'

Daily Herald

The fire started at 7:30 – it is believed, in a cloakroom in the Egyptian Hall and then in a quarter of an hour the greater part of the interior was ablaze, apparently aided by the presence of waxworks. Sir Henry Buckland took charge of staff fire-fighters.

An hour later the roof of the middle transept, scene of many famous concerts, fell in, burying the £9,000 organ, and flames shot to a height of 500ft., wreathing the ruins in white heat. Many birds and fish permanently housed there perished.

The Crystal Palace Orchestra, who were rehearsing in the Garden Hall – no exhibition was in progress – had thrilling escapes. They raced for their lives just before the roof crashed down.

Five hundred firemen and 100 fire engines were powerless; the entire London Fire Brigade was mobilised.

From time to time violent explosions shook the neighbourhood. An official of the Baird Television Company stated that 90 per cent of equipment in its laboratories near the south tower had been destroyed.

Daily Mail

Started Near Gas Container

'When I got to the office I found two of the three night duty firemen already at work with a high pressure hose.

'They did all they could, but the fire was very close to a big gas container. I cannot but think that the gas must have ignited early.

'Since 1913, when the Crystal Palace was taken over by a Trust, £300, 000 has been spent on improvements.'

Daily Mirror

THREAT TO SOUTH TOWER

Crowd Forced Back

The arched ironwork of the South Transept crashed at 9 o'clock. By this time outbuildings and stores round the base of the South Tower were blazing fiercely and, for the first time, firemen within the tower were pouring water on the flames.

Members of the Crystal Palace Orchestra, who were rehearsing in the Garden Hall lobby when the fire was discovered, had narrow escapes. Mr. W. H. Honnor, of Barnmead-road, Beckenham, said that they got out just before the centre transept fell. They had been rehearsing since 7.30p.m. At about 8.15 a girl employee told them that a fire had broken out, but that there was no danger.

Five minutes later one of the women members of the orchestra went out see if her car was safe. She returned to tell them that the Palace was well ablaze above the Centre Transept.

'We all ran to the entrance, on the left of the Centre Transept,' said Mr. J. Honnor. As I was getting out on to the parade, the front of the Centre Transept fell right out on to the road, in one great mass. We all had narrow escapes, and had a hard job to get clear.

'My car was left by the main entrance, and I ran along there to see if I could get it. As I did so, the transept fell, and my car was gone.

'Mr. F. H. White, the secretary also lost his car, which had been standing near mine.'

FULLY INSURED
TRUSTEE CLERK CALLED by 'PHONE

Mr. J. Wright Robinson, Clerk to the Trustees, was at a Masonic dinner when fire broke out.

'My wife 'phoned me, and I went straight to the Crystal Palace,' he said late last night. 'am now going to see Sir Henry Buckland, the general manager.'

The Crystal Palace, he added, was fully insured. Much had been destroyed which could never be replaced.   *Daily Telegraph*

CROWDS SEE CRYSTAL PALACE RUINS TODAY
Gas Explosion may have started blaze
DEBRIS EXPECTED TO SMOULDER FOR A WEEK

Sir Henry Buckland, general manager of the Crystal Palace, said to-day that 'We are insured, but not for anything like the value of the building,' He said, 'To build another Crystal Palace would cost between four and five millions. The site is in perpetuity for the nation and, of course, it will be utilised.'

Sir Henry said his theory was that the fire was caused by a big gas explosion.

'Nothing else in my opinion could have done it because it spread like lightning,' he said. 'We had dealt with three fires at the Palace and had never seen them spread as this one did. I think it originated somewhere in the north nave.

'It is simply terrible to see a life-work of 22 years humbled like this,' said Sir Henry, as he walked amid the ruins.

'There will never be another Crystal Palace. There can't be. Can you imagine any kind friend coming forward and volunteering to build us a replica?'   *Evening Standard*

STREAMS OF MOLTEN GLASS

Mr. A. Talbot, of Harold Road, Upper Norwood, employed in the Palace in a clerical capacity since before the war, told the News Chronicle, the fire had started in the centre section.

'I saw the whole thing,' he said. 'Inside the Palace the tiers of wooden seats and supports used in the concerts blazed up like matchwood. The steel frame bent and cracked in the furnace.

'Panes of glass in the roof, – they measure 30in. by 40in. and weigh as much as a man – buckled and melted in streams of molten glass.'   *News Chronicle*

WRECKED BY FIRE
The End of London's 'Play Palace'

He was walking towards the building with his daughter Crystal (named after the Palace) when he saw flames at 7:50pm 'We got to the entrance, and the fire was already raging across the roof… My firemen were there and they were doing all they could. I still hoped we could beat it. Fire engines were arriving all the time, but it wasn't long before I could see the building was lost.'   *The Star*

Transcript of magazines
£250,000 FIRE SWEEPS CRYSTAL PALACE
CROWDS AND MOTORISTS IMPEDE FIRE BRIGADES
HIGH WIND: 'LATE' CALL

The major portion of the famous Crystal Palace, on the south-eastern border of London county, was destroyed by fire on the night of November 30. Only the two flanking towers, and a portion of the centre of the building remain. Within are thousands of tons of twisted ironwork, lava-like glass, and debris. The fire was the most spectacular Londoners have seen for many years.

According to Sir Henry Buckland, the general manager, one of the Palace's private firemen saw the fire begin.

'A streak of flame ran along the top of the room and the place was ablaze in a moment. The time was 7.25 p.m. I thought at first that gas was the cause; now we know,' says Sir Henry. Penge Fire Brigade was the first municipal fire fighting organisation to be called. This was at 7.59 p.m.

There was a high wind, and only an average water supply in the mains. Sightseeing motorists checked the progress of reinforcing fire apparatus, and crowds of onlookers swept aside police cordons and hampered the firemen for a time.

The Crystal Palace, on the crest of Anerley-hill, erected about 1854, consisted of a large main building about 1,400 feet by 450 feet, with a large central transept and a smaller southern transept. It was constructed of a cast-iron framework, on which was hung wooden framing for the glass roof and sides. In height the building varied from 60 to 160 feet.

A number of galleries on each side extended the length of the building. These had wooden flooring and were supported by cast-iron stanchions. Access to them was provided by a number of broad wooden staircases. There were towers about 250 feet in height at each end of the building. That at the southern end adjoined the main building, but that at the northern was separated from the main building by an ornamental lake.

Another building, which adjoined the main building on the south side and extended for about 1,000 feet along Anerley-hill, was occupied by Baird Television, Ltd., which also occupied part of the South Tower. Altogether, the buildings covered an area of about 28 acres.

Overlooking ten counties, the Crystal Palace lies mainly within the area of the Penge Urban District Council. About 80 acres are in Beckenham; and the boundaries of London County Council and Croydon Corporation run through the front part.

At the request of Chief officer Goodman, of Penge, the senior officer of the London Fire Brigade assumed charge of the operations.

A strong nor'wester was blowing when at 8 p.m. Penge Fire Brigade called that of Beckenham. Simultaneously the West Norwood station of the London Fire Brigade was called, by street fire alarm. Telephonic calls followed.

114

Penge's motor pump was getting to work from a hydrant, at the north side of the centre transept, when Beckenham's two motor pumps arrived and connected with hydrants almost opposite the south transept.

London motor pumps, from West Norwood and Dulwich, started work, at about this time, from hydrants in front of the building.

Three minutes later – at 8.10, the centre transept collapsed, and the fire spread north and south, and the building began to flame from end to end.

The senior officer of the London Fire Brigade now gave a district call, followed, five minutes later, by a brigade call. Eventually the attendance of personnel and apparatus was:

BECKENHAM: Chief-officer J. H. P. Evans, M.I. Fire E., Deputy chief-officer Jameson – Two motor pumps, motor tender and 11 men.

CROYDON: Chief officer F. W. Delve, A.M.I. Fire E., – Motor pump, turntable ladder (fitted with pump) and 11 men.

LONDON: Major C. C. B. Morris, M.C. (in command). Commander A. N. G. Firebrace, Major F. W. Jackson, D.S.O., Messrs. C. M. Kerr and J. H. Fordham, assistant divisional officers, Supt. C. J. Wright, District-officer L. A. Shearman – sixty-one motor pumps, four turntable ladders, two tenders, two emergency tenders, nine lorries (two with hose), canteen van and 374 officers and men.

PENGE: Chief-officer J. Goodman – motor-pump and 8 men.

LONDON SALVAGE CORPS: Chief-officer J. H. Whiteman, Supt. W. J. Blyth – Three salvage tenders and 21 men.

Once the reinforcing motor pumps were put to work at hydrants, water supply began to dwindle, and, at 9 p.m. it was impossible, without a vacuum reading on the gauge, to obtain water for the four ¾-inch jets of one of the Beckenham pumps.

Recourse was had to water in an ornamental lake, near the North Tower, and by series-pumping, effective fire streams were provided for the front of the building.

Absence of fire-stops, and the shape of the building, enabled the wind-fanned fire rapidly to spread, and the efforts of the brigades were concentrated on preventing a collapse of the South Tower. In this, they succeeded, and the fire was halted 15 feet from the base of the tower!

A barrage of monitor jets, fed by 11 motor pumps drafting from the lake, saved the North Tower, despite the danger in which it was placed by the wind veering west.

Chief Evans' Views

'A remarkable feature was the absence of that great heat which one associates with large volumes of fire,' says Chief-officer Evans, who, prior to becoming chief at Beckenham was an officer at one of the busiest fire stations in London, that at Soho.

'Of course, the open nature of the building, and its surroundings, quickly dissipated the heat and so one could approach quite to the fire without discomfort.

'I have never seen a fire spread so rapidly; its progress could be seen by the reflected light.'

Other officers expressed similar opinions. One adds: 'The destruction of a building of such magnitude in so short a space of time, raises considerable doubt whether, in light of modern standards, it was a suitable structure for public entertainments.'

At 11.45 pm. Major Morris circulated the 'stop' message. By that time, a sub-officer and three firemen of the London Fire Brigade had suffered slight burns.

Throughout the night and next day, firemen were cooling down debris and extinguishing small re-ignitions, and, at 5 p.m., Supt. Wright, of the London Fire Brigade, left the smoking ruins in charge of Chief-officer Goodman, of Penge.

To enable the men of the three continuous-duty brigades to be relieved during the fire, Bromley Fire Brigade sent a motor pump and crew, and four-hour shifts were worked. The last motor pump and crew left the scene at 5 p.m. on December 3.

Among the countless sightseers was the Duke of Kent, who, accompanied by Major Morris, and Mr. E. Cruse, J.P., chairman of London's fire brigade committee, saw the various aspects of the fire.

LONDON F.B.'s RESOURCES

Working on the two-platoon system. London Fire Brigade had officers and men available, at the height of the Crystal Palace fire, to man the following apparatus to deal with other fires: Forty-one motor pumps, of which 39 had escapes, seven motor turntable ladders, and 12 motor tenders and escapes.

On the night of December 1, Major F. W. Jackson, D.S.O., gave a short broadcast, on the work of the brigade at the fire, from Broadcasting House, and the following Saturday evening, the first London fire-officer to arrive at the fire, Station-officer Hitchcock, made a further broadcast.   *FIRE magazine January 1937 (Reproduced by permission)*

DESTRUCTION OF THE CRYSTAL PALACE.

The following is an account of the Crystal Palace fire of 30th November taken from the official records of the London Fire Brigade.

The fire was discovered by a fireman employed by the Crystal Palace Trustees. The first call was received at West Norwood fire station at 8 p.m. At 8.10 p.m. a district call message was sent back from the fire, followed by a brigade call at 8.15 p.m.

The attendance from the London Fire Brigade was ultimately increased to 53 pumps, 8 dual-purpose appliances and 4 turn-table ladders (i.e. 61 pumping units), 2 emergency tenders, 7 lorries, 2 hose lorries, 2 tenders, 1 canteen van, 12 cars, 381 officers and men.

The attendance from other brigades was as follows: –

Penge Fire Brigade: One combination (pump and escape), 8 men.

Croydon Fire Brigade: One combination (pump and escape), 1 pump-ladder, 2 cars, 11 men.

Beckenham Fire Brigade: 2 pumps, 13 men.

There was a strong north-west wind blowing which veered to west at times.

The county boundary runs through the front part of the Palace, but practically the whole of the buildings are in the Penge area. The London Fire Brigade took charge at the request of the Chief Officer of the Penge Fire Brigade.

The Crystal Palace, which was erected on the crest of Anerley Hill about 1854, consisted of a large main building about 1,400 feet by 450 feet, with a large central transept and a smaller southern transept. It was constructed of a cast-iron framework, on which was hung wooden framing for the glass roof and sides. In height the building varied from 60 to 160 feet. A number of galleries on each side extended the length of the building. These had wooden flooring and were supported by cast-iron stanchions. Access to them was provided by a number of broad wooden staircases. There were towers about 250 feet in height at each end of the building. That at the southern end adjoined the main building, but that at the northern end was separated from the main building by an ornamental lake. Another building adjoined the main building on the south side and extended about 1,000 feet along Anerley Hill and was by occupied Baird Television, Ltd., who also occupied part of the South tower. Altogether the buildings covered an area of about 28 acres.

On the arrival of the first London Fire Brigade engines, the central transept was well alight, and within a few minutes the greater part of it had collapsed. Most appliances experienced considerable difficulty in approaching the fire owing to large crowds.

With no dividing walls to resist its advance and the strong north-west wind the fire spread rapidly. The length of the building also assisted the spread of the fire, involved the south transept and threatened to involve the South Tower and the building occupied by Baird Television. In view of the serious consequences which would be involved had this tower collapsed the main efforts of the brigade were directed to preventing the fire from spreading there.

Their efforts were successful, although the fire involved the television building and reached to within 15 feet of the Tower. As additional appliances arrived many branches were told to work on this side of the fire. With more pumps working, the water supply was proving inadequate, and pumping was resorted to. A number of pumps drew water from the ornamental lake by the North Tower and augmented the supply of those at work along Crystal Palace Parade.

With the wind veering west the fire began to spread in the direction of the North Tower also; and, in spite of jets being played on this side, within a short time little more than the iron structure of the northern section of the building remained.

At 11.45 p.m. it was possible to send back the STOP message. The duty was left and turned over to the Penge Brigade at 5p.m. on Tuesday, December 1st.

One sub-officer and three firemen were slight injured. They sustained burns from molten lead which dropped from the roof. *The Fireman, January 1937*

....

Looking back at the Crystal Palace by O. J. Morris

There is little need, I hope, to apologise for these notes on that lately-vanished landmark, the Crystal Palace.

This, then, was the fabulous place that suddenly disappeared from the Sydenham ridge between one sunrise and the next. A show of cats was duly advertised on the banner for the next day, and in fact, the cats were already being groomed in various parts of the country; this linen banner escaped unhurt, but very little else. The fire burned itself out on the west-side at the Palace turnstiles at the exit of the railway subway underneath Crystal Palace Parade. The fire consumed one of the huge wooden doors and started on the second.

The steps to the subway were covered in solidified molten glass and metal, an impressive reminder of the height from which they had trickled down.

At 9 a.m. on the Tuesday morning following the fire, flames were shooting here and there from the debris, and the burnt-out ground was hot enough, in places, to scorch one's boots. Just about here stood the great organ, one of the largest in the world, with its 3,714 pipes, and five miles of electrical conduit. Somewhere, too, in this mass of rubbish, is the exquisite model of an early American locomotive which so frequently attracted the enthusiasts of bygone days. Under the heat and the pressure, it is now probably a tiny lump of metal and brass.

Glass molten under the heat had contorted and trickled down to solidify into fantastic shapes. The panes were originally some 3ft long by 18in wide. These chunks are, of course, no longer glass, but an extremely brittle silicate, which crumbles at the slightest knock. Southern Railway Magazine, January 1937

The Crystal Palace Fire – The Station Master's Story

Mr. C. G. Allaston, Stationmaster, Crystal Palace High level, gives an account of the fire itself and various railway incidents connected with it.

"On Monday night, November 30th, the Crystal Palace was destroyed by fire.

It was a catastrophe of world-wide concern, and provided as dramatic and terrible a spectacle as this generation has witnessed. Swift, unerring destruction was the fate of the historic building, and two features in particular characterise its passing. One was the providential avoidance of the loss of human life, and the other the amazing rapidity with which the flames did their work.

Practically all that now remains of the massive structure which has occupied the site since 1854 is a desolate stretch of the blackened wreckage, with a huge tower at each end standing as sentinels over the ruins.

The blazing building could be seen for miles around and naturally attracted some thousands of people to the scene. The roads soon became so congested that many could not reach the scene because of the chaos along the roads. Fire engines were held up, and in one direction motor cars were lined back as far as Mitcham.

With a north-west wind grave concern was felt for the safety of the South Tower, which overlooks thickly populated streets of houses. As a precautionary measure, residents were warned to leave their homes. Heroic efforts were made by the firemen to save the tower, but it was not until close on 11.30 p.m. that their efforts had proved successful. The flames can best be described as like huge waves breaking against a lighthouse in stormy weather. For over a week after, the Crystal Palace Parade has been thronged with people at all hour of the day and night, many of them coming from distant places.

Thousands of pieces of glass were found in many roads some distance away – it is said a piece of metal was found as far away as Beckenham, having to be allowed to cool before it could be picked up.

The High Level Station entrance is situated on the Parade and faces the Palace. With the congestion it was most difficult for passengers to leave the station, and another exit was used in Farquhar Road. This soon became as bad as the main exit, consequently another, the footbridge, was used, well down behind the huge mass of people then gathered. This continued until the last train, 12.36 a.m.

Some 2,000 to 3,000 people stormed the Goods Yard, climbing up on trucks and steam trains standing out in the sidings, so many venturing near the live rails that it became necessary to send for our Police to control the crowds. Nothing could be done to get such a large number out, so they were permitted to remain, the position, by the way, giving an excellent view.

The London Fire Brigade made their headquarters in the south side booking office and waiting rooms, taking full possession of the National telephone until late in the afternoon of the next day. Just after 2 a.m. on Tuesday we were honoured with a visit by the Duke of Kent, who was very interested in the Brigade's methods and the arrangements in hand.

After the last train (11.27 p.m.) had left, about 70 passengers presented themselves for all stations to London, and a special was run at midnight to get them home. All had been so hemmed in with the crowd that some said they had been struggling for over an hour to get to the station.

In all there were 91 fire engines, 381 officers and firemen, from all parts ....”

Thousands of passengers were dealt with at both the High Level and Low Level Stations. During the week following, over 5,000 sightseers were booked away from these two stations. *Southern Railway Magazine, January 1937*

....

I SAW THE CRYSTAL PALACE BURN
By Sydney A. Legg

It was just after seven on a Monday night – November 30, 1936. My wife and I were about to start supper at our house on the edge of Crystal Palace grounds. Suddenly the back door was flung open by one of the three firemen on duty in the Palace. "Fire!" he shouted, then raced out again.

I ran to the Palace's main entrance, which I first used seventeen years before when I joined the staff from the army; now I was secretary to Sir Henry Buckland, the general manager. Beyond the entrance I could see flames breaking through a partition which separated the Palace itself from a block of single-storey offices. The north-west wind which had been blowing nearly a week was still strong.

In one of the nearby telephone boxes I rang the local London Fire Brigades. When I left the phone, the Egyptian Court was blazing. Flames were licking across the floor of the north nave as though it had been flooded with petrol. Great panes of glass were crashing down from sixty feet.

As I dashed along, opening gates for the fire engines, the crowds pushed in – cyclists, motorists, boys, girls, even women with prams. Dozens of streams of water were pouring on to the flames within a few minutes. Eventually there were ninety-five fire engines and 350 firemen at work.

It was useless. By now, the blaze was so great it was being watched 50 miles away at the Devil's Dyke, outside Brighton,

But the firemen did manage to reach the top of the South Tower and start a curtain of water streaming down all around the tower. They probably saved scores of lives. The tower stood on the edge of Anerley Hill, which was so packed with people and cars that no one could have retreated if the 280 foot tower had crashed.

My house – once a fire station itself in the days of horse-drawn vehicles – had the only telephone in the vicinity still working, and was turned into a headquarters.

When the water supply gave out, I led the firemen to the two-acre North Tower reservoir. Before long they had almost exhausted that.

By that time the fire was a fantastic sight and 8.30pm brought the most terrifying event of all. I was a short distance away when the whole of the great Centre Transept, 180 feet high and nearly a quarter of a mile long, collapsed, sinking slowly with a long continuous rumble.

At midnight the fire was still burning as strongly as ever. All through the night I was directing firemen to different places and answering what seemed to be hundreds of queries. I helped to rescue large bundles of documents – and dumped them in my bathroom.

Then, about two o'clock, someone brought in the early editions of the newspapers; only then, from the pictures, did we see how tremendous was the damage.

There were many theories about the start of the fire – even arson was suggested. I feel quite certain myself that it was due to a cigarette falling through a grating in the North Nave and being fanned by strong wind. The Palace firemen regularly put out small fires started this way. This time when the flames broke through, they were uncontrollable.

Illustrated, 30 January 1954

Crystal Palace Fire
Prompt action by the Gas company

Gas was neither the originating nor a contributory cause of the disastrous fire which reduced the Crystal Palace this week to a heap of ruins.

This assurance was given to THE GAS TIMES by the South Suburban Gas Company, in whose area the Crystal Palace is situated, and whose men were on the spot immediately the alarm was given.

One of the company's fitters, Mr. G. P. Chapman, who was per-manently employed at the Palace, heard of the fire unofficially and immediately returned there from his home and, on his own initiative and at considerable risk to his own life, turned off the inlet valves to the meters inside the burning building, thus preventing any escape of gas adding fuel to the fire before the supply was cut off from outside.

Main Supply Cut Off

Gas was supplied to the Palace through a number of service mains running from the parade in front of the building, each with a valve in the path outside, and these valves, together with the master valve for the 12in main running in the highway, were turned off well within an hour of the outbreak.

As soon as it was possible, the large water sealed meters measuring the supplies were examined and photographed, and they were found all to be perfectly intact with the exception of one which had sustained a crack, due apparently to a falling girder when the structure collapsed.

By what proved to be a fortunate coincidence, the members of the emergency squad were at the staff dance which was being held on the same evening as the fire occurred, and so they were able to arrive on the spot much more quickly than if they had had to start from their homes. Many of them, indeed, appeared on the scene complete in evening dress.

As a matter of fact, no official notification was received by the company, the news being brought to Mr. J. A. Gould, district engineer of the company, at the dance, by one of his assistants who happened to arrive late and consequently saw the commencement of the fire on his way.

Mr. Gould, who give us the above particulars, immediately left the dance with his assistants and proceeded with the stand-by lorry and emergency gang to the Palace; an learning of the speedy action taken, the brigade authorities were very relieved to learn that the gas had been so promptly cut eff.

Without comment

Sir Henry Buckland, general manager of the Crystal Palace, as reported by the *Daily Mail*:

"The cause? That is for experts to decide. I can only say I have an impression that the fire was started by gas. At any rate, I cannot think of anything else that would have produced such a tremendous blaze over such a great area in so short a time."

Sir Henry Buckland, as reported by the Daily Express: "A fused electric wire caused the fire. One of my staff spotted the fusing. It happened in an officials' rest room behind my offices, in practically the centre of the building. He saw a streak of flame running along the top of the room."

Progress magazine February 1937

Report by G. P. Chapman

In the February issue of "Progress", there was an account of the Crystal Palace fire, as seen from Crystal Palace Parade. Perhaps it would interest readers if I gave a description of the fire as I saw it from the grounds and the interior of the building itself.

I heard of the fire soon after it started, and hurried to the Palace, hoping to be able to shut off the main meters before the fire reached the positions in which they were fixed.

I passed through the Low Level entrance, into the grounds and proceeded to the north end, via the terraces. As I reached the lower terrace, the centre transept fell in, and broken glass, iron and blazing wood was thrown far out into the grounds. Millions of sparks were flying through the air, and I saw them ignite a fifty-foot flagstaff on the lower terrace and bring it crashing to the ground.

I then hurried, via Rockhills, into the north nave, and here, the scene was like a glimpse from Dante's Inferno. Huge columns and girders were crashing to the ground, glass was raining from the roof, and walls of flame were rushing along the building at unbelievable speed. The heat was unbearable and the noise deafening, but amidst it all, firemen were stolidly pouring thousands of gallons of water onto the blazing mass, as though it were all part of a day's work.

I was amazed, on going through the ruins later, at the damage done in so short a time. Not a vestige of the great organ, theatre, concert room, big clock, etc., was left. The debris consists, simply, of miles of twisted and distorted girders and pipes. The beautiful statues that adorned the building were simply masses of white powder and the Crystal Fountain smashed almost to pieces. The ornamental lake in the south nave was without water and dozens of goldfish were lying dead.

Of the many gas appliances destroyed, hardly any were actually affected by the great heat, but were broken by girders falling on them. For example, at the centre entrance, are five High Pressure Column Lamps on which the enamel canopies, globes and mantles are still intact. These lamps are fixed tight up to the main building, where the heat was greatest. This, I think, speaks well for the material and workmanship put into them.

George Palmer Chapman. 59a Tremaine Road, Anerley, SE20

The following letter was sent to Mr. Chapman on 12 December 1936.

SOUTH SURBURBAN GAS COMPANY

Chief Office, Lower Sydenham, SE26

Dear Sir

A report was made to the Directors at their meeting yesterday of your behavior on the occasion of the recent fire at the Crystal Palace, and they desired me to express their high appreciation of your splendid conduct and to make to you a special payment of £10, a cheque for which I have the pleasure in enclosing herewith.

Yours truly

Secretary

Bibliography

BOOKS

Beaver, Patrick
The Crystal Palace. Hugh Evelyn, London.

Beaver, Patrick
Memorable Fires in London. Post Magazine.

Bird, Eric L, M.C. A.R.I.B.A.
& Docking, Stanley J., M.A. ARCH, (L'Pool,) A.R.I.B.A., A.M.T.P.I.
Fire in Buildings. Adam & Charles Black, London.

Buckland, Sir Henry James
The Crystal Palace, (A descriptive booklet).

Chadwick, George F., M.A., B.S.C., P.H.D., DIPT, A.M.T.P.I., A.I.L.A.
The Works of Sir Joseph Paxton. The Architectural Press, London.

Kirk, Paul L.
Fire Investigation. Wiley, New York.

Kamm, Josephine
Joseph Paxton & The Crystal Palace. Methuen & Co Ltd.

McGrath, Raymond, Frost, A, C., & Beckett, H. E.
Glass in Architecture. The Architectural Press, London.

Morris, Major C.C.B., C.B.E., M.C., M.I.MECH.E.
Fire, E. Blackie & Son, Ltd.

Mosley, Sir Oswald
My Life. Thomas Nelson & Sons Ltd.

Markham, Violet
Paxton & The Bachelor Duke. Hodder, London.

Manchester, William
The Arms of Krupp. Michael Joseph, London.

Palmer, K.N.
Dust Explosions and Fires. Chapman & Hall, London

Wainwright, David
200 years of Toplis and Harding Group. Quiller Press Ltd.

Warwick, Alan R.
The Phoenix Suburb, (A South London Social History).
The Blue Boar Press, London.

30th November 1936 weather report. © Crown Copyright 1936.
Information provided by the National Meteorological Library
and Archive – Met Office, UK.

NEWSPAPERS

*Daily Herald • Daily Mail • Daily Mirror • Daily Telegraph
• Evening Standard • The Daily Express • The Dulwich News & South London Advertiser,
for February 14th, 1969 • The News Chronicle • The Star*

MAGAZINES

Fire, (The Journal of The British Fire Services, for January 1937)
published by Unisaf Publications Ltd., Tunbridge Wells, Kent

The Fireman (This is an old journal no longer in publication. originally published
by Merryweather & Sons Ltd, Fire Engineers, Greenwich, London.)

Engineering, Vol. CXI No.2887. Friday, 29th April, 1921

Southern Railway Magazine • Illustrated • Progress Magazine